FAULT

THE STORY OF WILLIAM STANLEY
A Self-Made Man

Eloïse Akpan

Eloïse Akpan

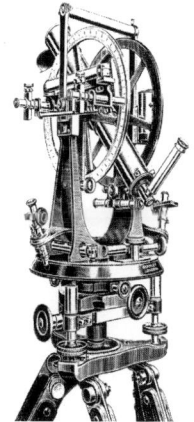

To Stephen, with best wishes. Sorry this is the last copy!
Eloïse

This book is dedicated to
Joe, Sophie, Lucia, William and Harvey

When Baptised.	Child's Christian Name.	Parents Name.		Abode.	Quality, Trade, or Profession.	By whom the Ceremony was performed.
		Christian.	Surname.			
1829. March 4 No. 513.	William Ford Robinson Son of	John Selina	Stanley	Holloway	Carpenter	Rev^d T Horn

BAPTISMS solemnized in the Parish of Islington in the County of Middlesex in the Year 1829

© Eloïse Akpan, Published 2000

Cover by Robert Dawson

Published by Eloïse Akpan, 28 Hurlstone Road, London SE25 6JD, U.K.
Printed by Sumner Type, London SE22

ISBN: 0-9538577-0-0

Acknowledgements

In this first attempt at research I have been most grateful for all the help received from Curators and Librarians and Keepers of Public Records in Croydon and in Central London, whose information is more readily and intuitively tapped than that in computers, which have to be asked exactly the right questions in order to be able to yield their riches. May we never, never, even begin to imagine that computers could replace such people!

Sincerest thanks, too, to Hugh Byford, whose name should, rightfully, also be on the title page, but who has preferred to leave that place to me alone. He is a proper Local Historian, did at least three-quarters of the research, and has also made valuable suggestions for amendments to the completed text, all of which have been gratefully incorporated.

Thanks, also, to the artistic and computer-literate members of my family who have given me help, advice and encouragement.

The 'Stanley' group of buildings at South Norwood

The Technical School The small Hall The Clock Tower The large Hall The Secretary's House

W. F. Stanley, Architect

CONTENTS

I	Who was William Stanley?	7
II	Childhood and Education	12
III	Employment	16
IV	Setting up in Business	20
V	Catalogues	26
VI	Move to Norwood	33
VII	Cumberlow	37
VIII	Retirement and Launching of Limited Company	44
IX	Death	54
X	Stanley's Heritage	58

Appendix 1: Some Inventions — 68

Appendix 2: Travel — 72

Appendix 3: Publications — 81

Wm. F. Stanley, 1909

Mrs 'Bessie' Stanley, 1907

I

WHO WAS WILLIAM STANLEY?

Almost a century after his death, the name of William Stanley is still a respected one, not only in South Norwood, the London suburb where the Public Halls and the Technical School next to them bear his name and usefully serve the community, but also internationally, wherever two or three precision instrument enthusiasts are gathered together.

The Halls cannot be said to be beautiful buildings, but they are bold and sturdy and they inspire affection for themselves and for their creator, because the materials used, marble, oak, teak, brass, as well as the workmanship, are of the highest quality and show that no expense was spared in providing the facilities to entertain and educate the local citizens.

It has been suggested that his main motive in setting up the Technical School was to provide a good workforce for his factory, but I think we have to allow that he was more disinterested than that. The Halls, for entertainment, were built first, and the school only started upon when he was well into his seventies and had already made his fortune and retired from active participation in the running of his factories. He, himself, had had a great struggle to get an education and his dream had always been to create better opportunities for the youngsters of the future, for their sake and for the good of the country, for he was an old-fashioned patriot, unquestioning in his belief that what was good for Britain was good for the world.

One of the factories which supplied the funds for these activities, near Norwood Junction station was still called the Stanley Works until it was partially destroyed by fire in 1998. Planning permission to redevelop it is conditional on the retaining of some of its distinctive features and it is hoped that the block of flats that it is to become will keep some reminder of its past in the name.

It would be hard to find a better example than William Stanley of the archetypal Victorian, one who embodied the whole spirit of the age. He was a self-made man, he was fascinated by all that was new and mechanical and that could be turned to advantage for himself and the Nation, he was optimistic, confident, extremely hard-working, public spirited and pretty sure that he was right. What an enviable state of mind! He did not have a large number of offspring to complete the picture of the typical Victorian Head of Family, but he adopted two and was a benefactor to his extended family of nephews and nieces. He painted water-colours, made wood-carvings, practised photography, interested himself in scientific matters way outside his own speciality, studied languages, travelled abroad, befriended musicians, served on school boards and wrote novels. He could be called Norwood's Renaissance Man.

Although Stanley did indeed pull himself up by his own bootstrings he had the inborn advantage of coming from a scholarly and able family. He inherited from his father, John Stanley, his engineering and technical talents, and from his mother's family, the Hickmans, the ability to turn them to financial advantage. Since the 17th Century, the Stanleys had been prominent people. As he says in his five lively autobiographical chapters which, sadly, only cover the first twenty years of his life:

Thomas Stanley, by permission of the National Portrait Gallery

Village school in the 1830s

The London Mechanics' Institution, home of Birkbeck College from 1824 to 1885, from a print at the College

I believe it is the accepted orthodox plan for a man who is going to talk much about himself to give some particulars of his more or less important forbears. Under these conditions I may state that my earliest ancestor of any note on my father's side was Thomas Stanley, of Cumberlow Green, Hertfordshire, a very learned classical scholar who wrote from 1600, after many minor works, his "History of Philosophy" which still remains a reference work. I am a sixth descendant - some of the Cumberlow property remained in the family until after my boyhood. A few of the direct descendants of Thomas Stanley were men of marked ability. My father was an engineer by intuition, and a splendid mechanic, so practical that he could do a fair day's work at many trades, but as a financial man he was a failure. Some of his patents are still worked, with his name attached as the inventor, though his death took place forty years ago. He never in his lifetime realized any profit from his inventions. He bore the character in life of an honest, active, unselfish man. My father married Selina Hickman, my mother, at twenty-four years of age, and he started in business as a builder. Being skilful, he had some success in having plenty of work and being well supplied with capital; but at his most successful period he appeared gradually to lose taste for his business, which did not afterwards receive much of his personal attention. On the other hand, he was always working out models and details for inventors, who were commonly very poor. After exhausting my mother's fortune, and through his business slowly failing, he was reduced to poverty...

On my mother's side, my great-grandfather, Edward Hickman, was an army and navy contractor, who supplied meat to the forces and amassed a large fortune. The most striking record I have heard of him was that he was very friendly with the Duke of York (son of George III) who was Controller of Contracts. This friendship, I was informed by my uncle, consisted for the most part in paying the Duke of York's gambling debts. Hickman left a numerous family equally well provided for, who, after his death spent the money he left in as respectable and easy a manner as possible.

The portrait, in the National Portrait Gallery, of Thomas Stanley (1625-1678), which is reproduced here with their kind permission, was formerly attributed to Sir Peter Lely, but in 1919 it was reattributed, rather less glamorously, to Gerard Soest. It is not currently exhibited but can be seen, by appointment, in the Gallery's stores in Merton. Thomas's great-grandfather was the 3rd Earl of Derby, who was Lord High Steward at the coronation of Queen Mary in 1553. Thomas Stanley was a very learned man, linguist and translator of poetry from Greek, Latin, French, Spanish and Italian who travelled a great deal and consecrated his life to study. His great works were the four volumes of his History of Philosophy and an edition of Aeschylus with Latin translation and commentary. He died in London on 12th April, 1674, and is buried in St. Martin in the Fields. He still merits an entry in the 15th edition of the Encyclopaedia Britannica, though William Stanley does not.

However, the latter has a long entry in the Dictionary of Business Biography, 1986, which considers his improvements to the

Theodolite his most significant invention. He could not be said to have invented it for the Egyptians had used the principle of the accurate measurement of triangles in building the pyramids. In the tomb of an Egyptian named Menna at Thebes there is a representation of two people surveying a field of corn with such an instrument and it had already progressed by the 19th century. However, Stanley's machine, with a rotating telescope for measuring horizontal and vertical angles and able to take sights on prominent objects at a distance, was an important improvement. He reduced the component parts from 226 to less than half that number, which made it not only lighter and cheaper, but more accurate. One of his Transit Theodolites is in the Whipple Museum in Cambridge.

The British Biographical Index 1998 quotes four further reference books[1] and The New Dictionary of British Biography, shortly to be published by Oxford University Press, will contain a 1000-word entry on him.

---

[1] Surrey Leaders, 1908, which also has a long entry including a portrait; A Critical Dictionary of English Literature, which refers to his Mathematical Drawing Instruments of 1866 and his Researches into the Properties and Movements of Fluids of 1881 and Who's Who in Kent, Surrey and Sussex, 1911. Geologists and the History of Geology by W.A.S. Sergeant, 1980, mentions his paper on the causes of earthquakes and volcanoes. The Divided Circle: A History of Instruments for Astronomy, Navigation and Surveying from Ancient Times to the Present by J.A. Bennett, Phaidon-Christies, 1987, which covers this vast subject in only 224 pages, finds room for pictures of two Stanley improvements, the Transit Theodolyte and the Reflecting Level.

II

CHILDHOOD AND EDUCATION

William Ford Robinson Stanley was born on 2nd February, 1829 in Islington and baptised there on 4th March of that same year by the Rev. J. Horn, in St. Mary's Church. At the time his parents, who had married in 1826, were living in a house on the site of the present Highbury Station.

His first two names were after his mother's brother, William Ford Hickman, who was his godfather, and one who took this relationship very seriously; later he gave the boy his start in life. The Robinson part of his name was dropped in adulthood after Stanley's cheque-book had been stolen and he changed his authorised signature as a precautionary measure.

The little boy's first memories were of staying with his paternal grandmother in Buckland, in Hertfordshire, but his parents' home was at Buntingford, four miles from Cumberlow Green, the ancient family seat. He was sent to the only village school in Buckland, where he was especially well treated because the vicar, a great friend of his grandmother, took an interest in his education. It was in this year that he learned 200 hymns by heart, but, more usefully, he also got such a good grounding in spelling and writing that he was able to continue his own education. This was as well because when he returned to his parents his schooling was erratic as neither parent thought it important that he attend. His mother kept him at home with his chilblains! This unpleasant swelling of the fingers and toes caused by the cold, which is mercifully virtually unheard of now, was suffered by many British children as late as the 1950s and the education of the nation would have been lamentable indeed if all the children with chilblains had missed schooling throughout the winter!

At the age of 10 he started going regularly to a day school, run by one Mr Peil, where, he says, he led "an idle life" and whose methods he describes:

> At this school the boys learned Mavor's spelling, reading, scripture, writing, drawing and were supposed to learn arithmetic. Of the last item, I may say, I remained at this school until I was twelve, and did not even learn the multiplication table, or any rule beyond addition, although in my ciphering book there were sums written down in reduction which I was supposed to have done. The cause of this was that the nephew of the master, who was styled arithmetical tutor, would never tell any boy how a sum was done, although by the pupil giving him a penny a week he would do them himself. If the penny was not forthcoming, the scholar was sent up to the master to have a "hander" - generally pronounced "'ander" - which was a sharp slap on the open hand with a leather strap. I feared the strap and paid the penny. The schoolmaster was particularly fond of the violin, which he practised in the school the greater part of the afternoon, when his nephew

was supposed to be giving arithmetic lessons, although more frequently he was playing "oughts and crosses" with the advanced pupils. In these afternoons the boys generally entertained each other in this manner, and I learned most interesting forms of paper-folding, puzzles and games on the slate. The only objection to this proceeding in headquarters was that if we made too much noise we disturbed the master's fiddling, and the "ander-strap" was thrown violently at our heads, and occasionally made nasty bruises. In my holidays, just before I was twelve years of age, I paid a visit to a maternal uncle, William Ford Hickman, who was my godfather. He passed me through an examination on my learning, in which I remember I could not state five figures in hundreds, thousands etc.

The result of this was that William Hickman offered to pay for his education until he was 14. The new school was only marginally better, the teacher, Mr Hatterley, a bank clerk who had previously been dismissed for drunkenness, sometimes being absent for days at a time on a drinking spree, and these experiences accounted for William's desire to build a school for boys when his circumstances allowed it in later life.

When he was 14, his father, being unable to pay his employees, insisted that William leave school and help him in his trade. This consisted of "joinery, smithing, plumbing, zinc work and other items of the building trade". At this time his maternal grandfather, who had been supplying his daughter with money, died, and the Stanleys then became seriously poor, sometimes hungry. His father, still inventing, made some important improvements in a weighing machine which he patented in 1855 and which were incorporated in all later machines and continued to be used long after the patent expired. He exhibited it at the Agricultural Society's show, and this led to the offer of a good job at £300 a year which he refused, preferring to struggle on his own. William described his father as "honest, active and unselfish" but these qualities did not make him a good provider, and the boy ran away from home to his uncle Hickman, who fed and clothed him and paid for some further education at the London Mechanics' Institution, now Birkbeck College. Shocked by this turn of events, John accepted the job offered him.

George Birkbeck must have had just such a person as William Stanley in mind when he created The Mechanics' Institution, in 1824. "England," he wrote "though the first manufacturing country in the world, is singularly deficient in schools for instructing the people in the Mechanical Arts. The principal object will be to make them acquainted with the facts of Chemistry and of Mechanical Philosophy and of the science of the creation and distribution of wealth". Stanley enrolled in 1843. Then, as now, the classes were in the evening and aimed at those in full-time employment and, apart from studying Engineering, he also delved into Phrenology. He was always interested in the different capacities of people and sought reasons for them.

III

EMPLOYMENT

A week after leaving home Stanley found a job with a drainage contractor, shoring up sewers at 15/- a week, but he was happy because he only had to work 10 hours a day, having been used to doing many more. He borrowed books from the Birkbeck library and, for the only time in his life, concentrated on poetry and read Shakespeare, Milton, Dryden, Byron and Shelley. After six months of this he got a shilling a week more as a Pattern Maker's Improver at an engineering firm in Whitechapel where his father worked. He soon moved up to a wage of 30/-, though, as it was discovered that he was good at wood-carving and he was set to making Gothic window frames for a country house. In his free evenings he and his father worked together and he learned to be a draughtsman, and he designed and made, at the age of 18, a wheel with metal spokes to replace the wooden one in common use on bicycles. This soon became the standard equipment. He wanted to try to patent it, but his father discouraged him, and in fact this would have been unsuccessful because the idea had, unknown to them, already been patented in 1826 by Theodore Jones, but this does not detract from the young designer's achievement.

When he was 20 he fell ill, and, attributing his illness to the unhealthy London air, he decided to return to Buntingford, where his mother's uncle, a Mr Warren, was glad to employ him. Mr Warren was a builder and had had to send to London when he wanted any ornamental work done in metal, wood or stone, but Stanley could do this on the spot. He put these years to very good use and writes:

> I often think what a glorious institution the observance of Sunday is, for rest from our daily occupations, in this country. When I first travelled abroad, where no observance of Sunday was made, I questioned the working classes upon the effect of constant daily employment throughout the year, and I found general condemnation of the system. As an instance, by an accident I lost a waterproof coat, and seeing all the shops open in Cologne I went in to buy one on Sunday, after 8 o'clock in the evening. A white-faced girl of about 20 years served me. I enquired of her about her holidays. She told me they were two days a year, Good Friday and Christmas Day. Her daily employment lasted from 8 in the morning till 9 at night. She said it was dull and lifeless. She thought England must be a very happy place, where shops were closed on Sundays. If she could get a day or a week off she thought it would make her very happy though she was sure she would sleep half of it away. I told her I hoped her country would one day see the value of Sunday for the people's good. Personally I owe all the success I have had in life to my Sunday studies (through which) I was raised financially above my competition.

During his years at Buntingford he set himself a rigorous timetable, with one subject to be studied seriously each year. In this way he improved his knowledge of English and became proficient in Astronomy, Geology, Chemistry, Maths and French, as well as Architecture and Theology. He set part of each Sunday aside for reading the Bible and the Scriptures of other religions. Of his French studies he says:

> I think it worth giving an account of the circumstances under which I completed this study. I took lessons from a Mr Fairchild who gave 12 lessons for one guinea. The first four lessons were on the sounds of the French alphabet. These were taught with diagrams of the mouth and throat and the students were made to see how these should be set to produce the French sounds... The teaching was so successful I never had a real difficulty with the language after the first lessons and was complimented by Frenchmen on my accent. When I first went to Paris I found I could speak the language easily without being misunderstood.

But Stanley was not the dull boy that "all work and no play" proverbially makes, and he could also turn his inventive mind to more frivolous purposes. One day he made an Aeolian harp and installed it in a girl-friend's grandmother's bay window to surprise her. A strong wind unexpectedly blew up and the horrific shrieks and groans emerging from the room terrified everybody. The only person brave enough to go in was the grandmother, who, armed with the poker, prepared to face whatever otherworldly creature was in there. History does not relate whether she used the poker on the offending object or its manufacturer, or, perhaps, both.

The local chemist was also interested in self-improvement and he and Stanley together created a Literary Society with a subscription of 5/- a year, which was spent on books to form a library which grew to 300 volumes. They were ambitious in their choice of guest speakers and on one occasion Lord Lytton came to address them on Pompeii. Despite this, Stanley began to feel that he was not getting enough mental stimulation in the country, and decided to move to London. By so doing he had to renounce the idea of taking a partnership in his uncle's firm, but they were not getting along very well, Mr Warren being made uneasy by the innovations his eager young nephew wanted to introduce, and Stanley preferring to be alone in business and manage things his own way.

He had always been intensely interested in Architecture and submitted a design for a competition in The Builder. Since he did not win, he concluded that he was not well enough equipped to become an architect and that engineering must provide his livelihood.

IV

SETTING UP IN BUSINESS

At this point Stanley's father made a useful suggestion. He had noticed how expensive mathematical instruments were, and that they were all imported from France and Switzerland, and thought that if they could be produced more cheaply in England there would certainly be a market for them.

Stanley had saved £100 from his high-paying job at 30/- a week and he found a shop to rent for 12/- a week at 3, Great Turnstile. The little alley-way leading from Holborn into Lincoln's Inn Fields still has that name, reminding us of the turnstile in question which was one of three revolving gates allowing foot-passengers but not cattle to pass in and out of the fields when they were used for grazing. Here, he proceeded to make his own mathematical instruments, T-squares, set squares, parallel rulers and French curves. He invented a new T-square which was an improvement on the standard one and which became universally used. As a sign of his trade he had a large T-square set above the door, but soon had to remove it because old ladies tended to think it indicated that he served teas! He worked extremely hard, and managed to make mathematical instruments and sell them but the country was in depression and trade was slow and he would have had to give up if his cousin, Harry Robinson, had not inherited £150 with no particular idea of how to invest it.

Great Turnstile, 1854, sketch by Ernest Mager Esq., FRIBA 1853, and today

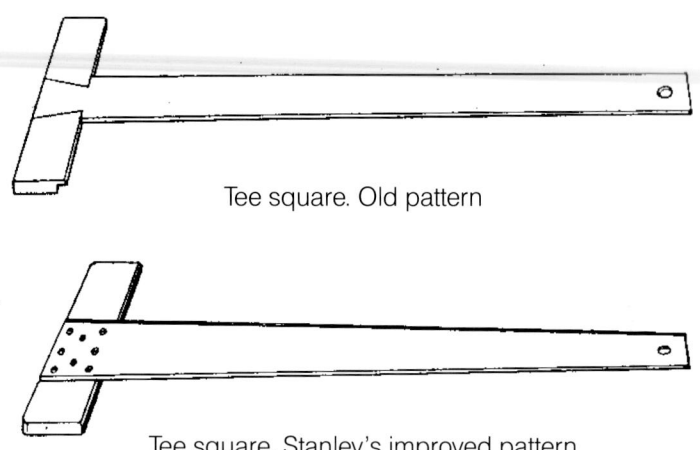

Tee square. Old pattern

Tee square. Stanley's improved pattern

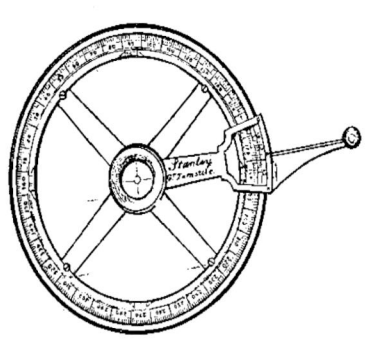

Circular protractor

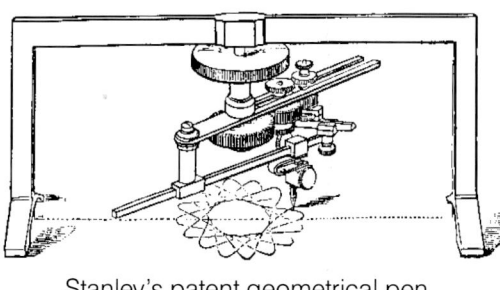

Stanley's patent geometrical pen

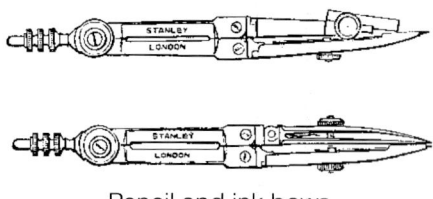

Pencil and ink bows

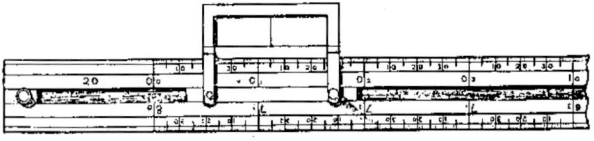

Improved computing scale

Stanley's old shop in Staple Inn, 1858

and today

Head Retail Department and Showrooms:
280 High Holborn,
London, W.C.

New branch of Surveying Instruments Factory, Garden Place, Lincoln's Inn Fields

With this added capital the little business was able to continue, but only just. He bemoaned the fact, as small businesses still do, that customers were slow to settle their accounts, thus adding to a struggling young firm's problems.

In Buntingford Stanley had fallen in love with a pretty local girl, Bessie Sutton and they were anxious to marry, but their plans were thwarted. Bessie and her widowed mother were dependent on an uncle for their income. This uncle came to London to examine Stanley and assess his "prospects". He was not persuaded that Stanley had any, and, unimpressed by the size or quality of the shop, said that if they were to marry he would stop Bessie's mother's allowance, which effectively put an end to their projects. It must have been a real love affair, for, although Bessie married a well-to-do farmer, she survived only two years and it was not until after she had died that Stanley felt inclined to look for another partner.

At the time there was a great fashion for stereoscopes, which were sold for 5/- each. Stanley discovered a simple method of making them which enabled him to sell them for a shilling. He called his invention the Panoptic. He received an order for 100 dozen of these from a wholesaler, so, after acquiring adjacent shops at 4-5 Great Turnstile, he then took better premises at 286 High Holborn and employed workers to make the toys. He did not patent this and it was soon copied all over the world, but it had served its purpose and provided him with the capital to get on with what he considered his real work, the manufacture of scientific instruments. 286 High Holborn is now a Wetherspoon's pub called Penderel's Oak, housed in a modern building, but one can imagine Stanley walking in Lincoln's Inn Fields, just behind, as changes there have been less radical, though his factory at number 5 no longer exists. In the Fields is a memorial to W.H. Smith, described as a "public-spirited and unselfish man". He was a contemporary of Stanley's, to whom the same description would apply.

The premises of another retail shop, in Staple Inn, are, of course, still there, in one of London's few surviving Elizabethan buildings.

Stanley's cousin had many friends and a busy social life, but he himself worked too hard for this to be possible, so he was lonely and set about looking for a wife. He met Eliza Ann Savory, a waterman's daughter, with whom, he later said "my life has been a uniform love-way". They were married on his birthday, 2nd February, in 1857 and lived to celebrate their Golden Wedding.

At the time of his marriage he regretted not having a nice home to take his wife to, for at first they could only afford to rent four rooms in Great Turnstile and live "above the shop". Cousin Harry lived with them until he died in 1859, thus leaving Stanley again in sole charge of his own business.

Harry died of consumption, as did so many young Londoners at the time, and Eliza Ann cared for him at home.

In 1861 Stanley made his own first important invention. This was an instrument which could divide any of the standard lengths of most nations into a number of equal parts very exactly, and it could expand or diminish the division down to the 200th part of an inch. This helped him to make instruments more precisely than his competitors could, so bringing in more business, and he received the first prize for Mathematical Dividing for his invention at the International Exhibition of 1862. A later version, manufactured in South Norwood, provided 300 divisions to the inch, so fine that a powerful lens had to be used to read them and it could be used on all the measuring standards known. All the principal topographical and railway works of the world at the time came to be undertaken with the help of this instrument. The patent certificate for this machine, along with the wax seal in a tin box then given to holders of patents was sold at Phillips, along with other patents, in December, 1999, for £550. Also offered for sale was a circular dividing machine, a much later model, made by George Dixon, who had learnt his trade from Stanley.

However, the work he did on that invention, after a long day, between 10 p.m. and midnight every night over several months took its toll and he fell seriously ill. The buildings at Great Turnstile were not healthy, so, after three months during which Eliza's nursing skills were again required, they moved to Kentish Town the next year. The move was not entirely helpful as he remained ill with gastric fever for most of 1862, but he managed to keep working. Here his much-loved and clever sister, Ann, joined them and proved herself useful in helping him with his literary and clerical work. This was becoming important as he wrote, and published himself, a book, <u>A Descriptive Treatise on Mathematical Drawing Instruments</u>, which became the standard work in its field and established him as the leading authority; it went into seven editions by 1900.

In 1862 he started to experiment with the use of the new material, aluminium, and to make his instruments of an alloy of nickel and silver, rather than the traditional brass, so they had the advantage of being lighter. He brought out the first catalogue of his products in 1864.

Stanley's own writing of his autobiography ends with the move to Kentish Town and the story is taken up by Richard Inwards, to whom Stanley left £200 in his will for the "trouble and expense he will incur in compiling editing and publishing my memoirs for which he has data". Inwards dedicates the book:

> To Stanley's widow, his adopted children, his relatives, fellow managers and workmen and to the masters and scholars of the Technical Schools, this short and meagre account of his life is dedicated in the hope that the influence and example of the good man gone may be of use in encouraging others who would tread in his steps and achieve successes similar to his own.

He himself regrets that he cannot equal Stanley's lively style, though he faithfully records facts and has included an invaluable calendar of events which facilitated further research[2].

One of the first stories Inwards tells is rather pious and Stanley would probably have hesitated to tell it of himself, or, perhaps, not have thought it worthy of note, but it is interesting because of the light it throws on the times and on his philosophy.

He had an order which required one small item that he could not make himself, but he undertook to have the whole instrument ready for his customer by a certain date. The craftsman who would

---

[2] There are few copies of this book extant but two are to be found in the Croydon Local Studies library, one donated by W.F. Stanley & Co. and the other by H. Keatley Moore in 1911.

From an original design for a book cover by H. Hardcastle, aged 16.
A *Stanley* Scholar, 1910

Stanley's first straight line dividing machine

Stanley's first circular dividing machine

make this item lived three miles away and on the day agreed, after his normal shop hours of 6 a.m. to 9 p.m., Stanley walked over to collect it. It was not ready. He went the next evening and the next until he retrieved it for his customer. The item cost sixpence, of which his profit was twopence halfpenny, but he was always intensely conscious of deadlines and believed that success in business depended on meeting them. He had learnt this from his uncle, who was always prompt with deliveries and was successful in business. His father, inherently a much more talented man, was not realistic about time and never made money.

Stanley thought that he and his uncle could be said to be lucky men and his father an unlucky one, but that their luck was only in their inherited gifts - the rest was hard work and what he called "tact", a consideration of the customer. His axiom was "A man makes his own luck".

On August 31st of 1865 Stanley's father died and was buried in Highgate Cemetery, having lived long enough to see him on the way to success.

V

CATALOGUES

There is a book in the library of the Science Museum in London called Handlist of Scientific Instrument-Makers' Trade Catalogues, 1600-1914, by R.G.W. Anderson, J. Burnett and B. Gee, published by the National Museum of Scotland, in which W.F. Stanley Ltd. figures importantly. The authors drew up this list because they realized the usefulness of trade catalogues in identifying and dating instruments for historical purposes. Stanley's catalogues give a wonderful picture of the growing enterprise over the years; a book could be written on them alone, so it is good to find that samples of them have been collected by the British Library and were carefully bound in 1980.

Anderson et al. say that the introductory material provides evidence concerning the relationship between the maker and his customers, and this is certainly the case with Stanley's catalogues, many of which contain a letter addressed to his clients explaining his aims, his achievements, and his difficulties. The 5th edition, for example, was prefaced by these delightfully Stanleyesque words:

> Gentlemen: In offering to your notice a new edition of my catalogue I beg to call attention to a few particulars of my manufacture. When I commenced business as a shopkeeper in 1854, being a practical workman I manufactured the articles made with my

Telegrams: 'Turnstile, London.' Nat. Tel. No. 188 (Holborn)

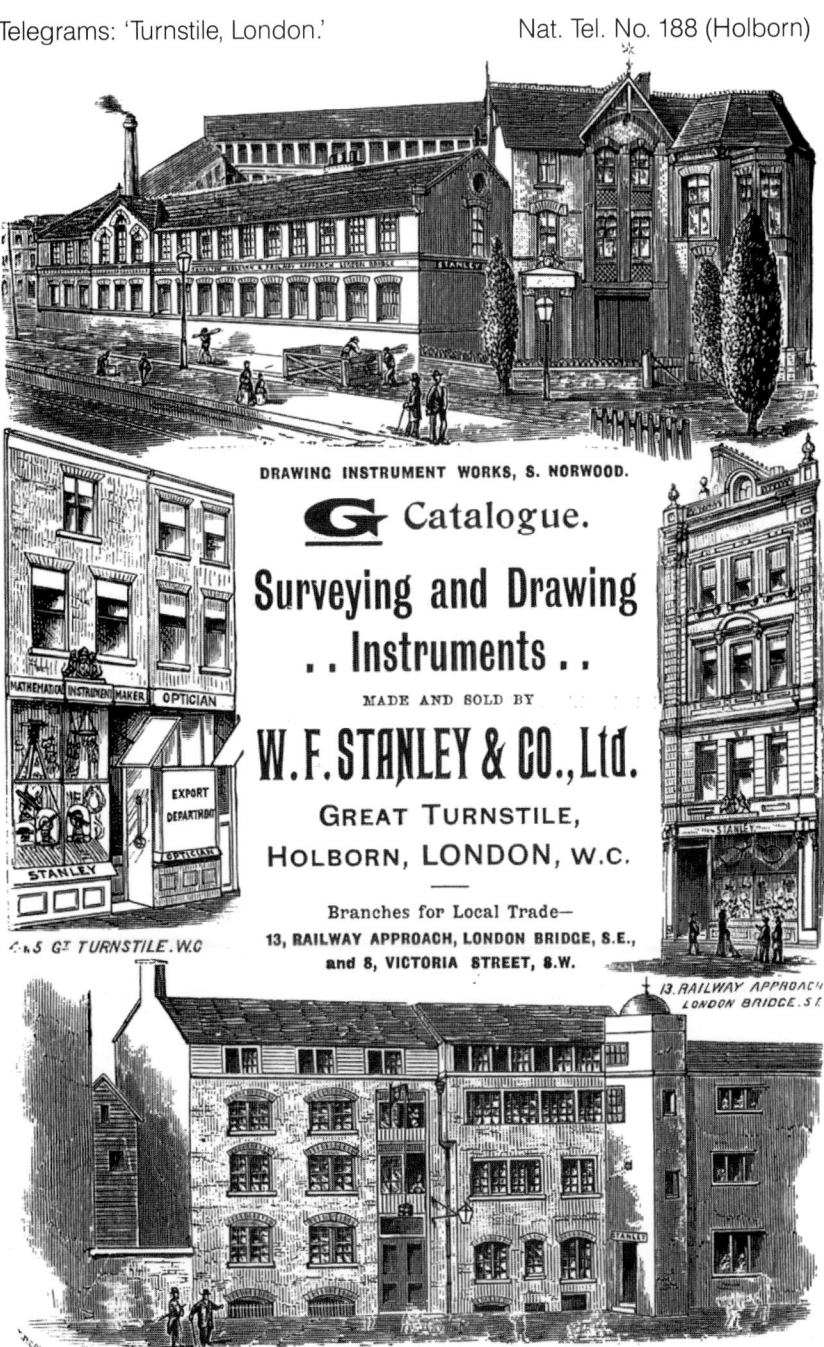

DRAWING INSTRUMENT WORKS, S. NORWOOD.

G Catalogue.

Surveying and Drawing .. Instruments ..

MADE AND SOLD BY

W. F. STANLEY & CO., Ltd.

GREAT TURNSTILE,
HOLBORN, LONDON, W.C.

Branches for Local Trade—
13, RAILWAY APPROACH, LONDON BRIDGE, S.E.,
and 8, VICTORIA STREET, S.W.

Surveying Instrument Works, Tichborne Court, W.C.

Drawing Instruments, as Improved by Stanley

own hands. I now employ one or more workmen for each especial branch of the business, which is entirely under my own care. This enables me to be confident the work is properly done, my object being to attain perfection in every branch of the business, both in accuracy and finish, so as to be able to give entire warranty that the commonest article sold shall entirely answer the purpose for which it is intended. Mention is made of these facts, as it is the present custom in London for brokers and second-hand instrument makers to style themselves "makers" of whom I never knew one to be a maker.

Rather, I beg to call attention to the many improvements I have made in Drawing Instruments, in construction, form and general accuracy. The leading position these improvements have taken is an assurance that they have been found useful. Recently I have felt compelled to Patent my improvement as I found my ideas were copied by the trade before I had time to perfect them....

The extensive patronage of very large orders I have received from the Government during the past year have induced me to construct machinery for the manufacture of a large part of work that could only be performed imperfectly by hand labour: this places the quality of some of my instruments beyond competition.

In conclusion, I beg to thank those gentlemen whose kind recommendations have secured me the largest manufacturing mathematical business I believe in the country.

I am, gentlemen, your Obedient Servant, WFS

Terms: Cash without discount. Goods can be had from the manufactury only. No country agents. Business Hours: 8 a.m. to 7.30 p.m., Sat. 8 a.m. to 5.30 p.m.

At the back of the catalogue is an impressive list of customers, including several government departments, the Army and the Royal Navy, railways at home and abroad, London University and others.

The 10th edition, in 1870, shows slightly reduced Saturday opening hours, 8 a.m. to 3 p.m. and includes a map to enable customers to reach the shop.

By 1881 the catalogue contained 3000 items and there was a staff of 80. The 1890 catalogue has a large section on Magic Lanterns, running on oil lamps, with an enormous selection of sets of slides which could be either hired or bought. These include views of beauty spots world wide, the siege of Paris, the Russo-Turkish war, the overland route to India, the travels of Dr Livingstone, Scripture History (photographs!), the Life of John Bunyan, Dante's Inferno with illustrations by Doré and countless improving stories such as Mother's Last Words and The Drunkard's Children, but there were also purely entertaining ones for children.

DISSOLVING VIEW APPARATUS.

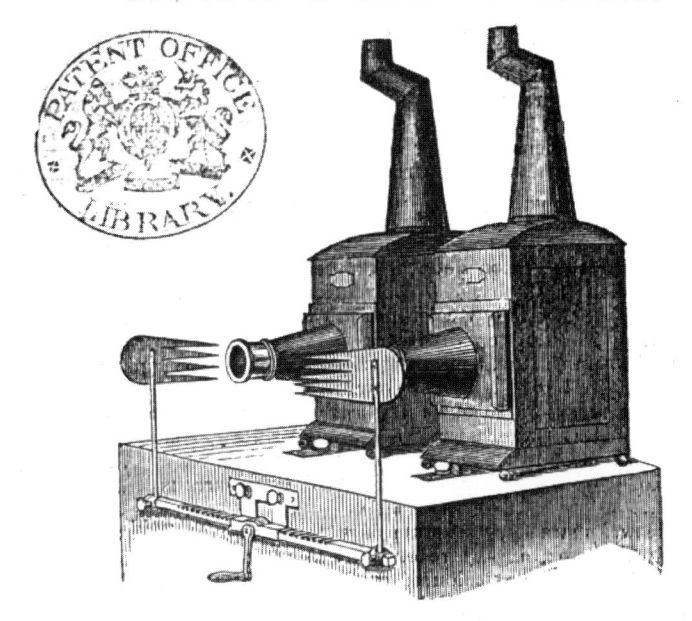

Dissolving view apparatus

Slides only, for Magic and Phantasmagoria Lanterns

IN ALL CASES WHERE OFFERED IN COMPETITION
:: :: FOR DESIGN AND QUALITY OF WORK :: ::

Stanley's Instruments

HAVE COME OUT — **THE HIGHEST.**

MEDAL,
Highest Award for Mathematical Instruments, International Exhibition, 1862.

MEDAL,
International Exhibition, 1873.

MEDAL,
Highest Award, Melbourne Exhibition, 1880.

GOLD MEDAL,
International Inventions Exhibition, 1885, for Improvements in Mathematical and Philosophical Instruments.

GOLD MEDAL & DIPLOMA
For Mining Instruments, Mining Exhibition, Crystal Palace, 1890

NINE GOLD MEDALS,
Paris Exhibition, 1900.

GOLD MEDAL,
St. Louis Exhibition, 1904-5, for Surveying and Mining Instruments, &c., &c.

THREE GRANDS PRIX,
Franco-British Exhibition, 1908, for Surveying, Mathematical and Scientific Instruments respectively.

GRAND PRIZE,
Japan-British Exhibition, 1910, for Surveying and Drawing Instruments.

GRAND PRIX, DIPLOMA OF HONOUR AND GOLD MEDAL,
Brussels Exhibition, 1910, for Surveying and Drawing Instruments.

FOUR GRANDS PRIX AND DIPLOMA OF HONOUR,
Highest Award, Turin Exhibition, 1911, for Surveying and Drawing Instruments.

GOLD MEDAL,
Allahabad Exhibition, 1911, for Surveying and Drawing Instruments and Appliances.

In 1891 Stanley writes:

Gentlemen: ... My trade is divided into many branches, for which I have special workmen. 17 of these branches are carried on in my own works, in which over 130 workmen are constantly employed. For the remainder of the work sold by me, I employ chamber-men, who work at their own homes. ... In this manner I had them made until 1873. With honourable workmen, my patterns were sacred, and my ideas fairly carried out. But these instruments were *never sold* by me in the state that they left the workmen's hands. For the first four years of business those sold were examined and corrected by myself. Onward from this time I trained others to do this technical work. Since 1874, from the necessity of obtaining a quantity of uniformly good work to meet demands, I have made all the working parts of surveying and drawing instruments by machines.... My machinery for dividing mathematical work and scales is now driven by steam power, which produces greater accuracy and regularity of division than I was able to produce formerly by hand work. With acknowledgment of past favours and kind recommendation, I am, Gentlemen, your obedient servant, WFS.

1893's edition includes a page on the postal arrangements and charges internal and world-wide and the details of an enviable bus service: from Fenchurch Street to Great Turnstile, every 10 minutes, 2d., from Liverpool St, every 5 minutes, 1d, from Paddington, every

5 minutes, 3d. and so on, with taxi fares from 106 different parts of London - from one shilling from Charing Cross to two and sixpence from Clapham Common. Stanley meant his customers to find him without difficulty. The mountain had to come to Mahomet!

By 1903, when it reached its golden jubilee the firm had become "the largest business of its kind in the world". In 1908 it is claimed to be "working under the same management of our Mr. W.F. Stanley" though this was not strictly true as he had handed over to his brother and his long-standing colleague, Henry Tallack, by then, but obviously his name was an important asset. At that time the firm's products were being pirated and customers were urged even more urgently than in the past to purchase direct and distrust anyone claiming to be an agent. Many of their orders came by telegraph and they had an elaborate coding system to save expense, with each item in the catalogue having a code name and also codes for delivery instructions.

The 1924 catalogue, the 31st, is a very lavish one, on better paper, and was actually sold for 4/6d. H.T. Tallack was then the Managing Director, and the working hours had become 9 a.m. to 6 p.m., and Saturdays 9 a.m. to 1 p.m. There were agents in 21 foreign countries on all five continents.

In 1999 an 8-page note on Use and Adjustment of The Stanley G.S.378 Precision Level of c. 1950 and a Stanley Allbrit Planimeters Catalogue, 11 pages, also c. 1950 were each offered for sale on the Internet. It is probably safe to say that Stanley would have been among the first to appreciate the uses of the Internet.

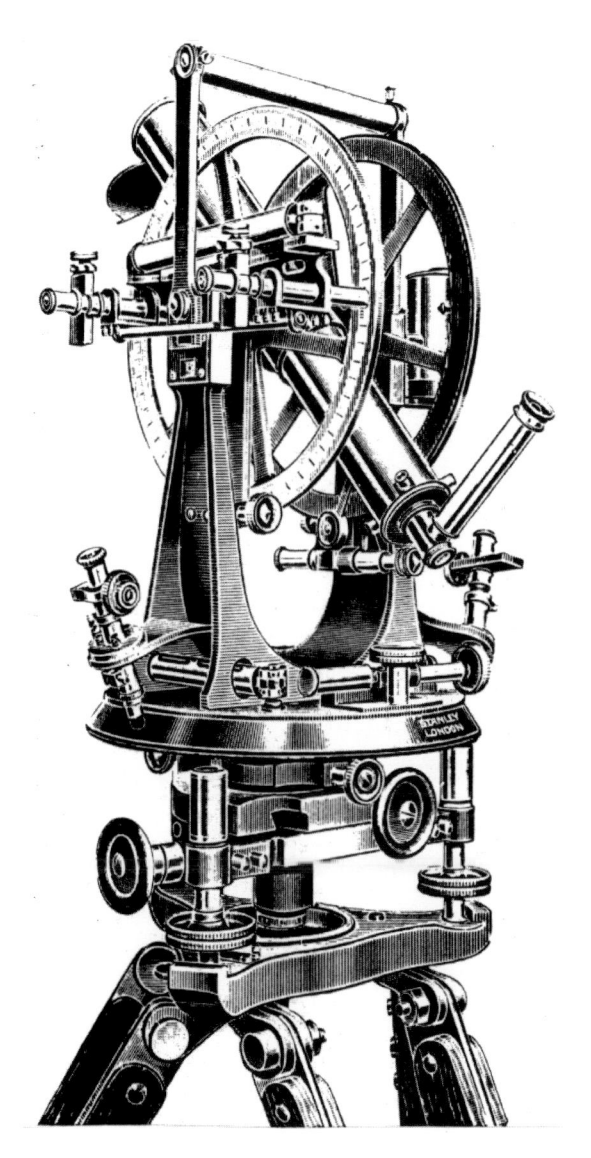

Stanley's Improved Theodolyte

Slide Rules for Calculation.

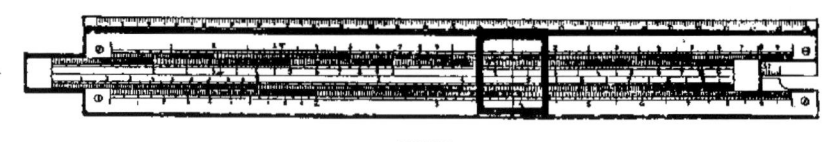

CJ1556

CJ1556	Slide Rule, 10 inch, mahogany, faced with celluloid on both sides to prevent warping, marked with Logarithmic scales of numbers, squares and square roots, sines, tangents, and scale of equal parts. Suitable for all ordinary professional calculations and giving most results in three figures. Of best make, with glass cursor, complete in card case with instructions for use	$3.65
CJ1557	Ditto, 5 inch, in case, with book of instructions	2.10
CJ1558	Ditto, 14 ,, ,, ,, ,, ...	9.40
CJ1559	Ditto, 20 ,, ,, ,, ,, ...	15.60

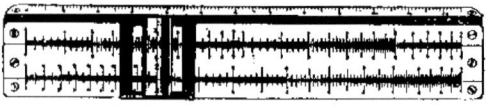

New 5" Pocket Rule with Magnifying Cursor.

CJ1560	Slide Rule, 5 inch, as above but with magnifying lens to the cursor, in case, with book of instructions	$3.40
CJ1561	Ditto, 10 inch, ditto, with instructions, no case	5.10

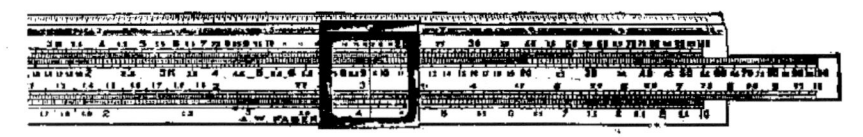

One end of CJ1562

CJ1562	A. W. Faber's Slide Rule, 10 inch, of similar design to the above, boxwood faced with celluloid, in card case	$3.65
CJ1563	Ditto, with 50 page book of instructions	4.20

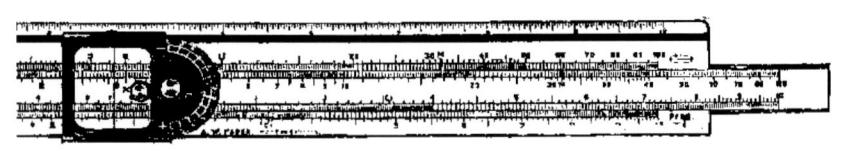

One end of CJ1564

CJ1564	A. W. Faber's Improved Rule, with digit registering cursor, 11 inch, in case	$4.20
CJ1565	Ditto, with book of instructions	4.85
CJ1566	Nestler's "Rietz" Slide Rule, 10 inch, having scales of cubes, and logarithms on the face, in addition to the usual scales, in case, with book of instructions	4.75
CJ1567	Nestler's "Precision" Slide Rule, with instructions and case	7.00
CJ1568	Solid Leather Case for 10 inch slide rule	0.90
CJ1569	,, ,, 14 ,, ,, ,, ...	1.25

Books on the Slide Rule and how to use it, Hoare, $0.90 ; Pickworth, $0.70 ; Blaine, $0.90

To produce all these instruments he acquired factories at 5, Lincoln's Inn, where the first metal drawing instruments were made, at Tichbourne Court, off Holborn for surveying instruments and the Optical division, at 13, Railway Approach, London Bridge. On 7th December, 1999 a Deed Box belonging to Stanley containing 53 leases, agreements, etc. including a lease between the Wardens of St. Saviours, Southwark and William Ford Stanley dated 5th April, 1865 for a Warehouse East side of Tichbourne Court, High Holborn, was auctioned at Phillips, Bond Street, London, and bought by the Science Museum for £700.

As well as paying so much personal attention to the administrative side of his business Stanley was busy inventing and took out more patents at a great pace: no. 226 in 1863 - a drawing instrument for drawing circles or arcs from 2 to 200 feet radius, later imitated by most other instrument-makers, no. 644 in 1866 containing descriptions of several instruments including one for depicting the forms of the teeth of gear wheels, no 3335 in 1867 emerging from his interest in predicting the weather - a Meteorometer for recording wind direction, pressure, temperature, moisture and rainfall all in one instrument. He installed one on the roof of his factory on the London Bridge railway approach, and, much later, another on the tower of the Stanley Technical School, no longer, unfortunately, *in situ*. Presumably he just nipped around to the Patent Office in person to hand in his applications, as it was conveniently close in Southampton Buildings, off Chancery Lane, though the splendid purpose-built edifice that stands there now would not have been used until after Stanley had moved to South Norwood.

Sometimes 78 patents are attributed to him and sometimes 79. The discrepancy is because, in 1885 he proposed to make an application for a patented Tooth Injector, but this was never followed up. The records, therefore, show no description or sketch of this, so we are left to imagine what it might have been. He also published books on his inventions. Even those allergic to lists will surely be fascinated by the variety of the subjects this polymath put his mind to, and it's impossible to do him justice without detailing his later inventions (see Appendix 1), most of which were patented. These patents are now kept at the British Library in beautiful leather-bound books with gold-engraved coats of arms on the cover and can be examined on application by anybody interested.

At the International Inventors' Exhibition at Wembley in 1885 he received a gold medal for his productions. In fact, he seems to have invented almost everything **but** the famous Stanley knife! Nor was he responsible for the other familiar Stanley hand tools which are manufactured by a completely different company.

VI

MOVE TO NORWOOD

It was in 1867 that Stanley was doing well enough to move his home and business to the Norwood hills which, particularly since the opening of the Beulah Spa in the previous century, had been a favoured spot for those wishing to leave the polluted London air. He made his first attempts at architecture and designed his own house, or rather a pair of houses, "Stanleybury" and "Cumberlow House", 74 and 76 Albert Road, and his factory, listed in the Croydon Directories in the 1876 edition as "Stanley Mathematical Instruments", near Norwood Junction station. The houses were in fairly standard Victorian style but with some of the characteristic Stanley adjuncts such as the heavy window surrounds he liked to incorporate. They were more imposing than the other houses in the area and on a more generous plot of land, giving room for an unusually large front garden.

The factory was a substantial enterprise, for the equipment was produced from start to finish there, right from the casting of the ingots of metal to the manufacture of the most delicate instruments. The metal, silver, brass, gunmetal or aluminium was first molten in the foundry and then passed to the machine room and transformed into complete sets of drawing instruments by expert workmen. The elaborate, felt-lined boxes for storing the instruments were also made on the premises, so skilled cabinet-makers were employed. Oak, mahogany, walnut and rosewood were used. Raw materials came from all over the world and the products were exported as far afield as Canada, India and Japan. South Norwood was, indeed, a hive of industry in the second half of the 19th century. By 1889 Stanley was supplying all the principal government departments with precision instruments and employed 150 men. The front door of the Sales Office has an engraved marble plaque over it announcing proudly "CONTRACTORS TO H.M. GOVERNMENT, COUNCIL OF INDIA, ADMIRALTY". Another nice little Stanley touch is the engraved marble notice with the prosaic message "Sales Office. Visitors kindly ring for attention". The Company manufactured there until 1926, when the enterprise was transferred to New Eltham.

With his business prospering, Stanley was now able to devote more time to his hobbies. He took up painting and resumed woodcarving, and became proficient enough at this to give a preliminary class at the St. Mark's Hall. A carved, inlaid tray he made was exhibited at the Stanley Art Exhibition Club which was opened in May, 1904. Probably he did not himself carve the Four Ages of Man on the door of the Stanley Hall, but it was the kind of work he appreciated and liked to commission. He also painted his own and his wife's portraits in oils. Perhaps these were not very good - none of the present family members know of their whereabouts and one wonders if, like Lady Churchill, who destroyed a hated portrait of her husband by Graham Sutherland, Eliza disposed of them after his death.

He became a magistrate and sat on the Croydon Bench on Mondays and Saturdays. This was not something he enjoyed for he was rather tender-hearted and hated punishing boys for stealing apples.

Stanley was a member of the Royal Metereological Society and often addressed the members and contributed to their Journal. In 1876 he read them a paper on Clocks, in 1882 he gave another on the Mechanical Conditions of Storms, Hurricanes and Cyclones. In 1884 he spoke on "Certain effects which may have been produced in the atmosphere by floating particles of volcanic matter from the eruptions of Krakatoa and Mount St Augustin" and in 1885 on a suggested improvement in radiation thermometers. In 1886 he spoke to them on "Three years' work with the chrono-barometer and chrono-thermometer" and the following year they had an exhibition of his barometer with rising and falling index and his snow gauge. These two instruments were then presented to the Science Museum and are still there, though not on open display.

These events were reported in the Quarterly Journals of the Society between 1877 and 1891, which are now preserved in the National Meteorological Library and Archive at Bracknell in Berkshire.

In 1882 he was elected a member of the Physical Society of London and read them a paper on Forms of Movement in Fluids.

In 1883 he gave a paper to the Geologists' Association on Earth Subsidence and Elevation, and went with them on a field trip to Bangor. They made him a Fellow the following year and in 1885 he went on a further expedition to the Ardennes and River Meuse.

The appended list of books will also give some idea of the breadth of his interests, but, for him, being interested in something meant also trying to improve it, and usually succeeding. He explored how to grow wood particularly intended for paper manufacture, for example, and researched the causes of earthquakes and eruptions.

    When he retired from the Bench one of his colleagues commented that there would be no more £10 notes put in the poor-box.

VII

CUMBERLOW

The couple had no children of their own, but in 1877 had adopted Eliza Ann, Stanley's brother Edward's daughter when she was nine years old. Another family custom was to give almost everybody but William nicknames and Eliza Ann became Lilie (pronounced Lylie). The feeling among present members of the family is that, in keeping with fairly common practice in Victorian times, because William and Eliza's marriage had not been blessed in this way it was probably considered only right and proper for a brother to "give" them one of his children. Brother Edward and his wife, Maria, did in fact have five children, three girls and two boys, so perhaps they decided to hand over the third girl.

The following year a family friend and his son were drowned in a shipwreck off the coast of Spain and the mother of the remaining child did not feel able to raise her alone. Maud Martin, then aged seven, was being cared for by the Stanleys who were going to equip her with the clothing required for admission to an orphanage, but they became so fond of her they decided to adopt her instead. She had a very happy childhood there, considered Bessie, as Eliza came to be called, her mother and had no further contact with her natural one. Later she changed her name to Stanley. Later still she married a German resident in Britain and became Maud Jaeger. (One cannot but wonder whether Eliza knew that Bessie was the name of William's original love.)

The family impression is that Lilie, though not Maud, was rather spoilt by William and Bessie and she grew up to be imperious and bossy. It was Maud, though, whom William described in his will as "my sweet companion".

On 23rd January 1894 Lilie married Dr Robert Lachlan Pinkerton and they lived in a large house at 25 South Norwood Hill where she ran a household of the "children should be seen and not heard" variety. Visiting children, such as, later, great-niece Anne, remembered, after having been received in the drawing room, being banished to a room at the top of the house where there was no heating and with no possibility of escape. This house is still there, but has been converted into flats. There are attic rooms, close under the roof, and, although the roof area has been rebuilt in order to make more flats, it only needs a little imagination to see wan faces peering down from the windows!

Maud and Lilie had a fine, large and interesting house to live in, as in 1878 Stanley had bought six acres of land at the foot of the old "Beggars' Hill", by then South Norwood Hill, on a patch of clay soil previously occupied by Pascall's brick and tile works and built himself a tall, solid mansion, with his characteristically stone-framed windows. High under the roof can be seen the Stanley coat-of-arms, a buck's head, adapted perhaps from the arms of his illustrious ancestors, with the motto "sans changer" because he believed in steadfastly pursuing a goal until it was achieved. As the area became developed and imposing houses were built along the road its ancient name, with its unfortunate connotations, became unsuitable for the address of the respectable families inhabiting it and in 1864 it was renamed, prosaically enough, South Norwood Hill. Fortunately, because Lily Langtry lived there, later, at White Hall, and it would

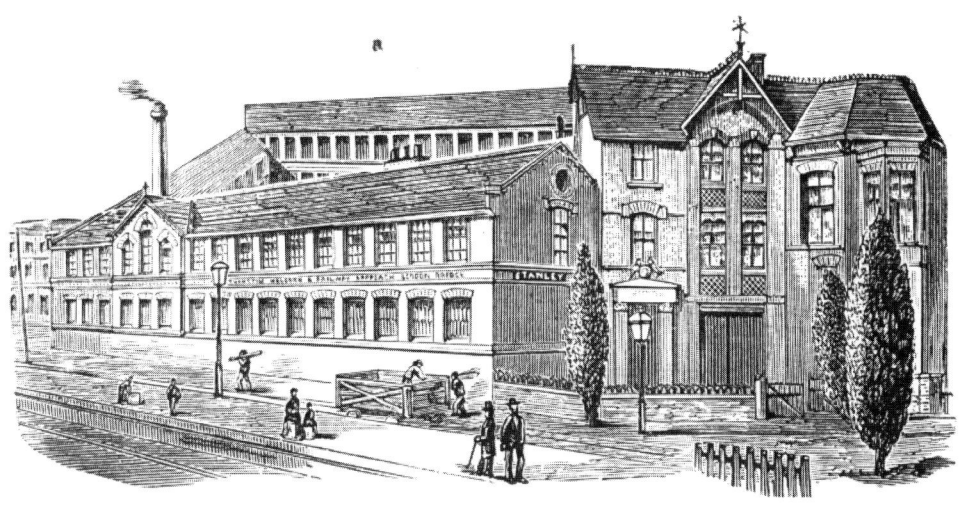

Drawing instrument works, foundry, and saw mills, South Norwood, in its heyday. . .

. . . and just before the fire

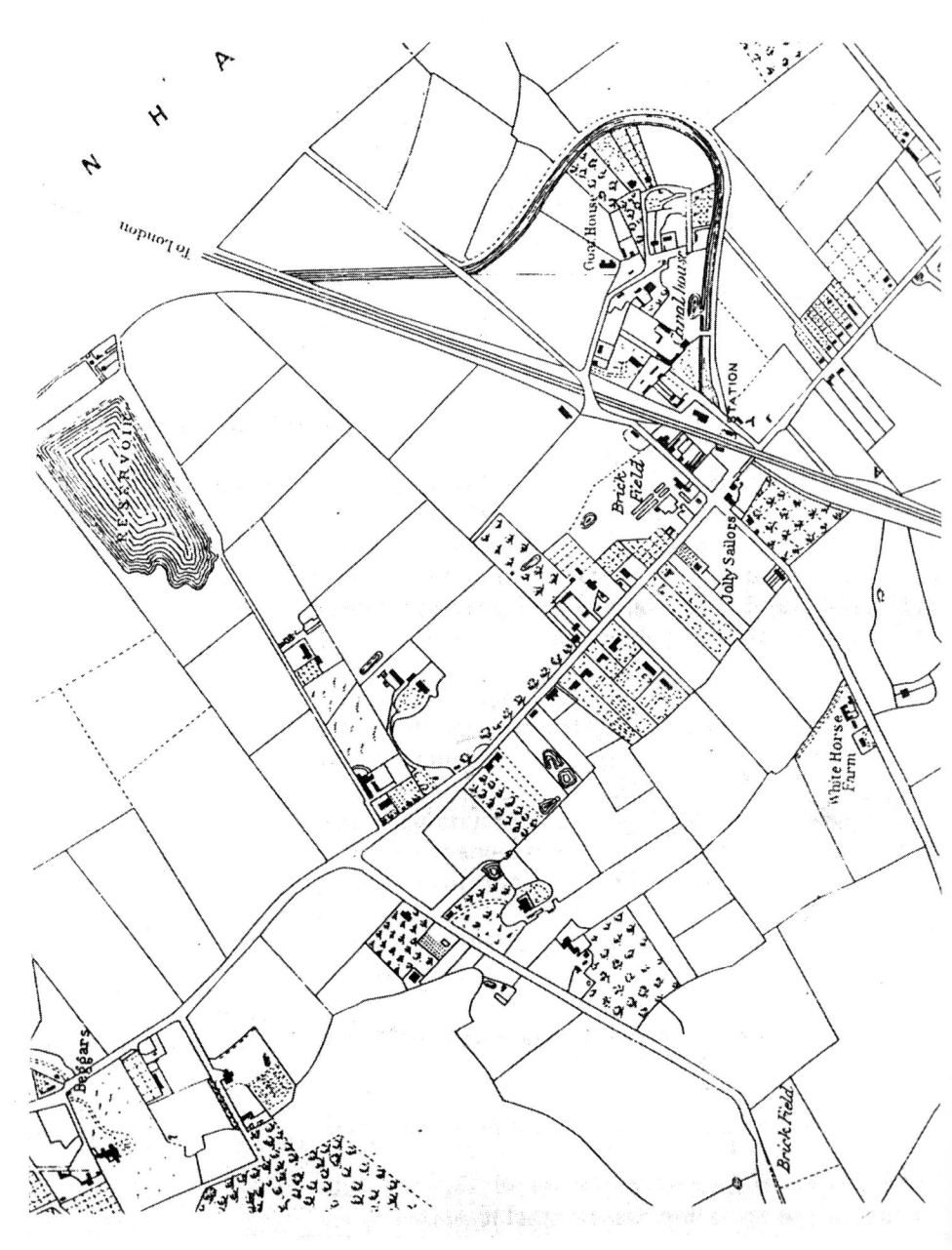

Robert's plan of the Parish of Croydon, 1847

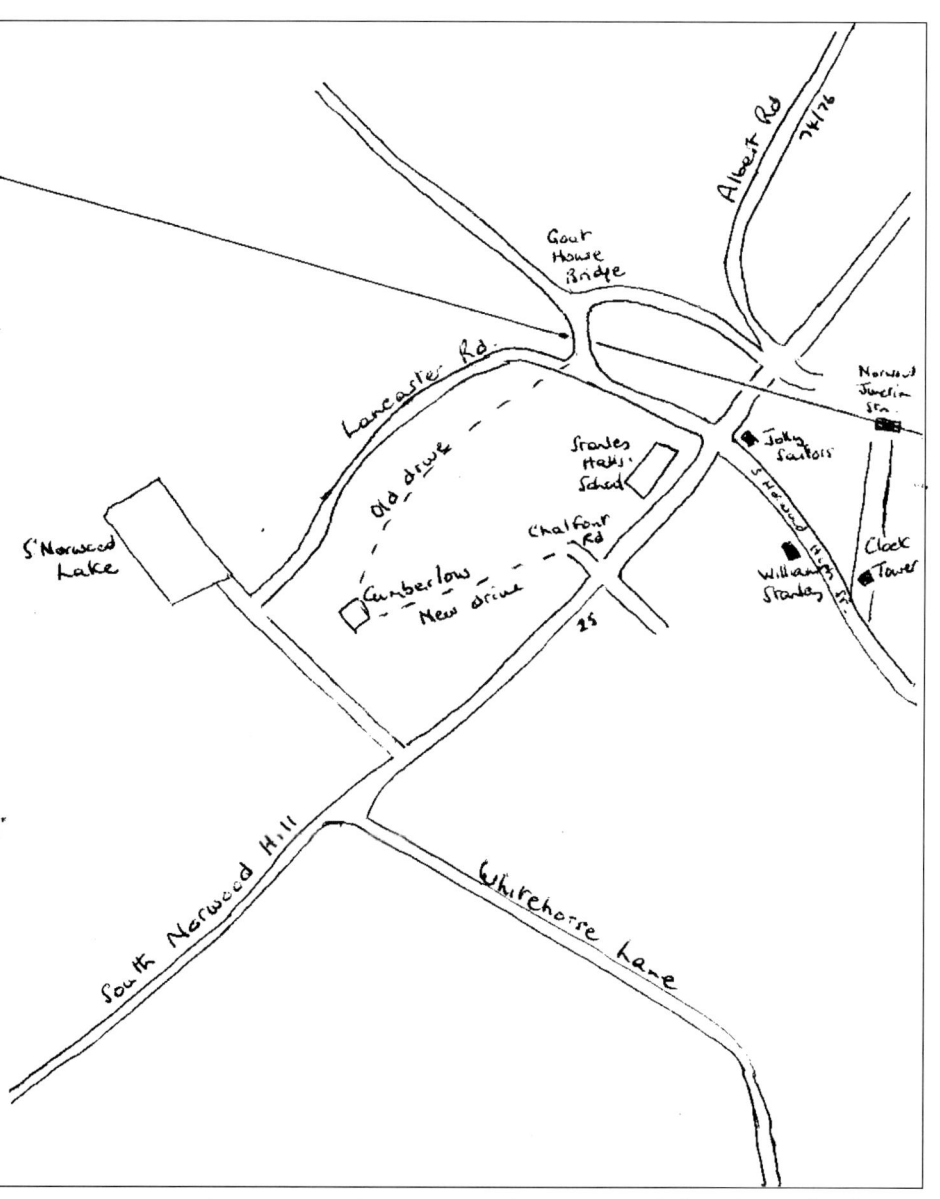

1847 Plan Updated to show places mentioned in text

Stanleybury

Cumberlow

hardly have been acceptable for King Edward VII to visit her in "Beggars' Hill"!

Ahead of his times, as usual, Stanley developed what we now call a brownfield site and the desolate area was transformed into a landscaped garden filled with carefully-selected plants. He designed the house himself, naming it Cumberlow in recognition of his origins in Hertfordshire. The postal address of the house was, originally, 1, Lancaster Road, from which a long drive led past a gate-keeper's lodge to the house. This entrance has not been used for fifty years or more and the gate is padlocked and in a sad state indeed, derelict, graffitti-covered and litter-bestrewn; the lodge was demolished in the 1990s, despite protestations by the Croydon Society. Number 3 is now the first number in Lancaster Road and from its garden the old drive can be seen winding its way up to Cumberlow through the trees.

Opposite the site of the lodge is Goat House Bridge, a reminder of a house of that name belonging to the Archbishop of Canterbury. Possibly it was a hunting lodge, since the Great North Wood was a favourite area for deer hunting, and "Goat House" was a disrespectful, local name for Deer House. It is rumoured to have been one of the many houses for which it is claimed "Queen Elizabeth slept here". It is certainly known that she went hunting in the area. The present entrance to Cumberlow is via Chalfont Road, off South Norwood Hill.

Family life was full of activity. Stanley liked to write plays for everyone to perform and they had their own private family theatre company which they called The Theatre Loyal. In 1883, for example, they put on a play called "A Slight Mistake" in which four

Miss Stanleys took part along with a Mr. Charles Kirtle. Stanley himself painted the scenery. Lilie and Maud took part in many of the performances at the Stanley Halls.

Painting in water colours was another family hobby and music was important too. Sister Ann was a good pianist and used to play for them, but she died rather soon, in 1877, much missed. Maud had a pet cat which fell out of a top-floor window and survived and Stanley claimed that his dog could understand 50 different words. He was very fond of animals and refused to eat veal, having seen, in childhood, a young calf being daily bled so that its meat would remain white. The gardener was instructed to leave some of the cherries unnetted so that the birds should have their fill.

On the face of it, Bessie, adored and depended on by William and with all the comforts that money could buy at her disposal, still confided to her niece at the end of her life that she had three wishes which were unfulfilled - to have a low house (Cumberlow is disproportionately tall), to have children, and to again see her sister, who lived in India.

Stanley left Cumberlow in his will to the Council to be used for the benefit of children. It was sold on 16th March, 1911, for £4,200 but it has always been used as an institution for children. In 1963 ownership was transferred to the London Borough of Lambeth and for a time the child murderer, Mary Bell was housed there until local residents protested and she was removed to Wales. Now, under the name of Cumberlow Community, it provides a home for 15 deprived children where they also receive their education and any treatment they require. The number is deliberately small so that there is the feeling of a family. The house has been greatly extended but

Cumberlow with some of its present family

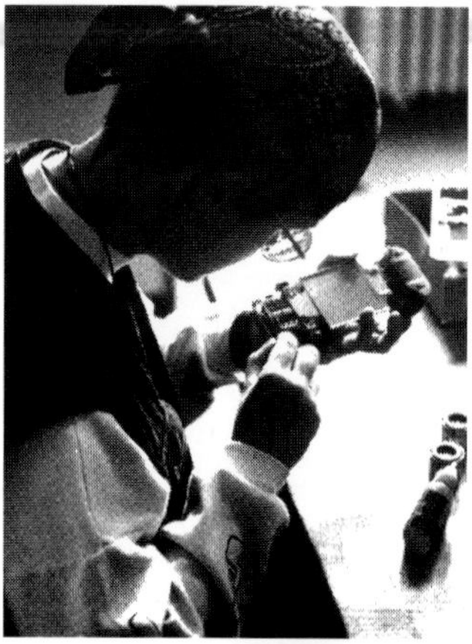
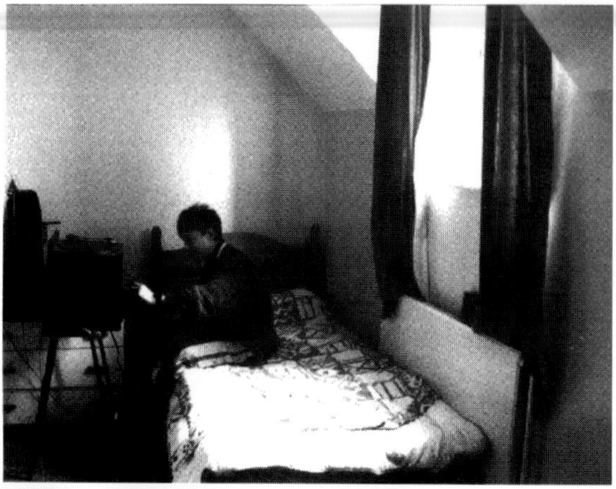
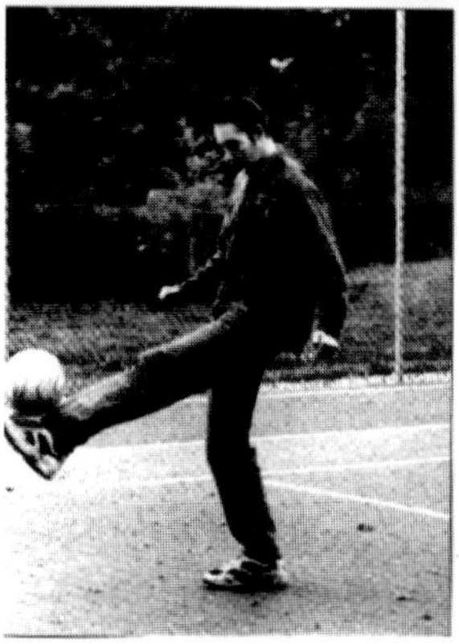
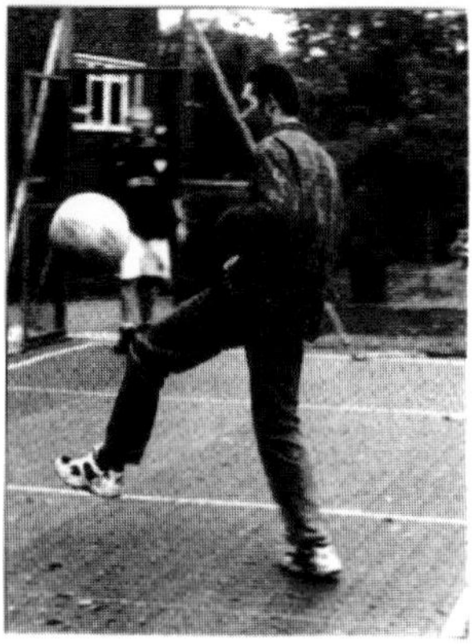
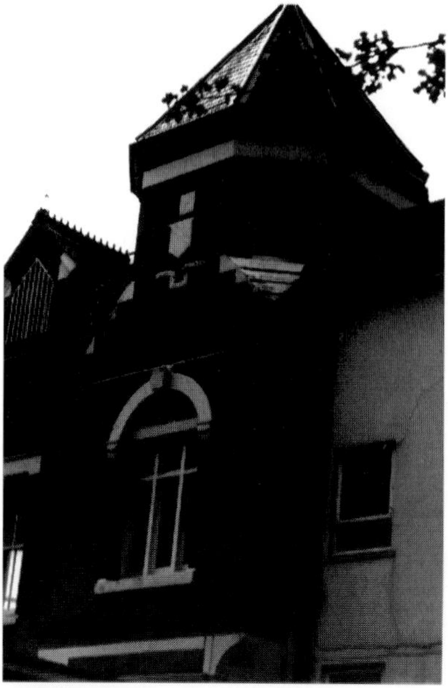
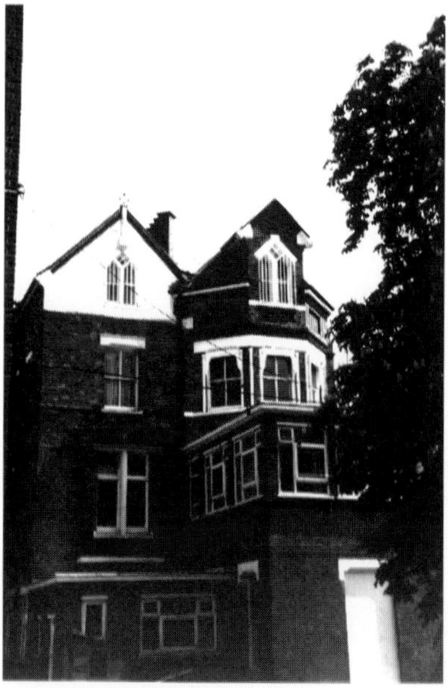

the main part of the building still shows Stanley's architectural style. Although tiles are no longer made on the site it is somehow satisfying that in an adjoining road there is still Boyden's Tile Warehouse.

Under the 1870 Education Act, Board Schools had been created and in 1873 Stanley became a member of the Croydon School Board, as education was a subject very close to his heart. When, later, the Education Committee was formed the local Boards were abolished and he never ceased to regret this. The Act made education compulsory for children up to the age of 14. It was free, but a penny a day was charged for dinner. For some families this was not affordable, so Mrs Stanley ran annual concerts at which the artistes, including, of course, the indefatigable Maud and Lilie, gave their services free, to raise money for a fund for the Stanley Penny Dinner Fund. One of these concerts raised £40 - expenses were £8, leaving £32, and 32 times the 240 pence there were then in the pound paid for a good many dinners.

On 23rd January 1881 Stanley's mother, Selina, died, having seen him become rich and a famous man in his field and his community.

In 1884 Stanley wrote the first of many letters to the English Mechanic, this one on the Area of the Oceans of the World. An eminent doctor from Göttingen had estimated the area of the oceans as 231,915,950 square miles but Stanley claimed that this was a greater surface area than that of the whole globe and that the correct figure was 112,295,750 square miles. It is easy to imagine how much Stanley would have enjoyed the English Mechanic for it discussed and described every mechanical innovation and new scientific theory of the time, with diagrams and illustrations. He wrote to them on buffers, on heat conductors, on the luminiferous ether, on carbon atoms, on the rotation of the planets, on his theory of cometary matter, on the ice age, on whether the universe is finite, on spontaneous generation and matter, and the magazine, of course, had articles describing many of his inventions. In 1900 he wrote on a subject which has again been a matter of discussion at the turn of the millennium. Then as now there was a dispute as to whether the 31st December 1899 was the last day of the 19th Century, or whether, in fact, the century could not be said to be complete until 31st December 1900. A Fellow of the Royal Astronomical Society had written claiming the latter date was the correct one but Stanley writes:

> One scarcely feels comfortable in differing from so logical an authority as a Fellow of the Royal Astronomical Society, but I really find it difficult to accept his argument ... that there never was a year 0. It strikes me that when Christ ... was born, that this must have been his first year, and if we wished to express his age in terms of the year, say, at 3 months old, we could only do this by putting 0 years 3 months. After Our Lord was one year he entered his second year ... and after a period of 100 years from 0 we entered the second century, and so, on Monday 1st January 1900 we entered the 20th century.

With money worries far behind him, there was the possibility of foreign travel and the couple went to Italy, France and up the Rhine to Switzerland. They were accompanied by their extended family, a bevy of young nephews and nieces, for they liked to share their good fortune, but most holidays were spent in the English country-side, painting watercolours. A well-recorded holiday took place in the spring of 1889 when they went on a three-month cruise on board the Jaffa through the Straits of Gibraltar and the Mediterranean. Stanley sent letters at weekly intervals to the Norwood News describing their impressions. A few extracts (Appendix 2) below show Stanley in holiday, and often amusingly ironic mood, but they are also interesting because they provide a window on history in the making. For example, they visited Naples before and after the Unification of Italy in 1870. In 1872, before this transformation of Italy from a collection of city states to a modern European country had had time to manifest itself, the Stanleys had found a picturesque port with traditionally-clad people living in mud huts and fishermen's boats pulled up haphazardly on the quay. Seventeen years later another visit revealed a city under construction, inhabitants in modern European-style dress and the fishermen banished to a distant part of the bay.

VIII

RETIREMENT AND LAUNCHING OF LIMITED COMPANY

On April 20th, 1900 W.F. Stanley & Co. Ltd. was launched with 25,000 shares of £5 each and it was this money that was used for the building of the Halls and the School. Although Chairman of the Board and Managing Director, Stanley now left the operation of the company to Henry Thomas Tallack, his collaborator of many years standing and his brother, Joseph, and spent his time on his public work and writing.

His first big public work was the construction of the Stanley Hall, which he projected in December 1901. It is a fine theatre with its marble pillars, its tiled walls, its elegant balcony and teak roof beams reminiscent of the hull of a ship. In fact it is said that these were obtained from a ship-builder's yard, seen there by Stanley on one of his visits in connection with supplying instruments for the Royal Navy. The busts outside were meant to emphasise the fact that there should be no political or sectarian bias in the plays presented: Gladstone and Beaconsfield for Politics, Darwin and Faraday for Science and Dickens and Tennyson for Literature. The bust of Stanley was the work of his niece, Lilie Stanley. Unfortunately all these busts were stolen in the 1960s and the niches remain empty. A statue of Vulcan was evidently too big for the thieves to transport and

Details from Stanley Halls

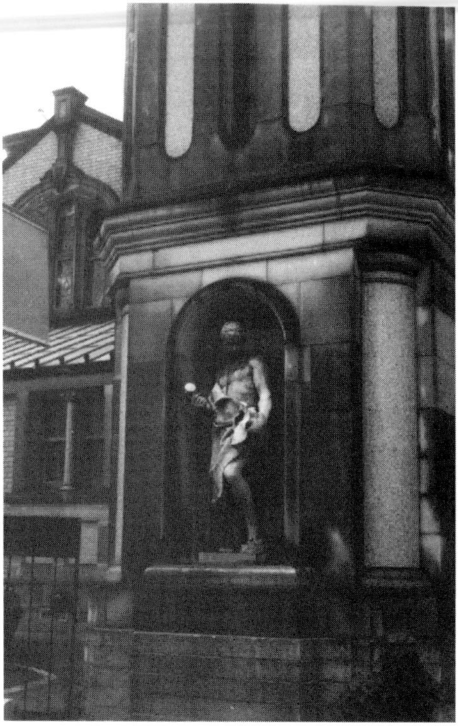

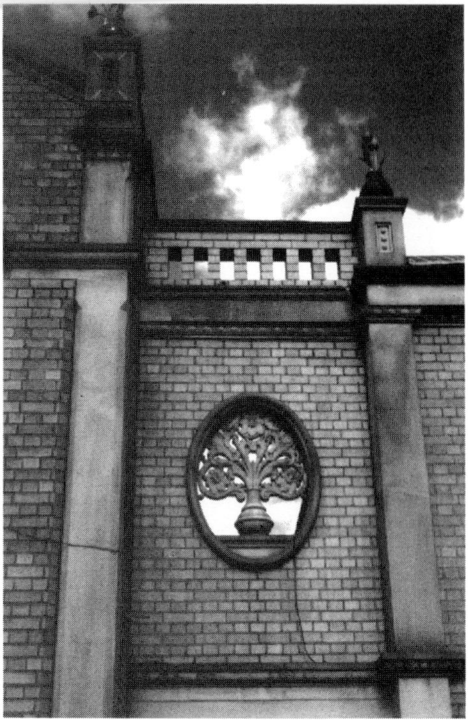

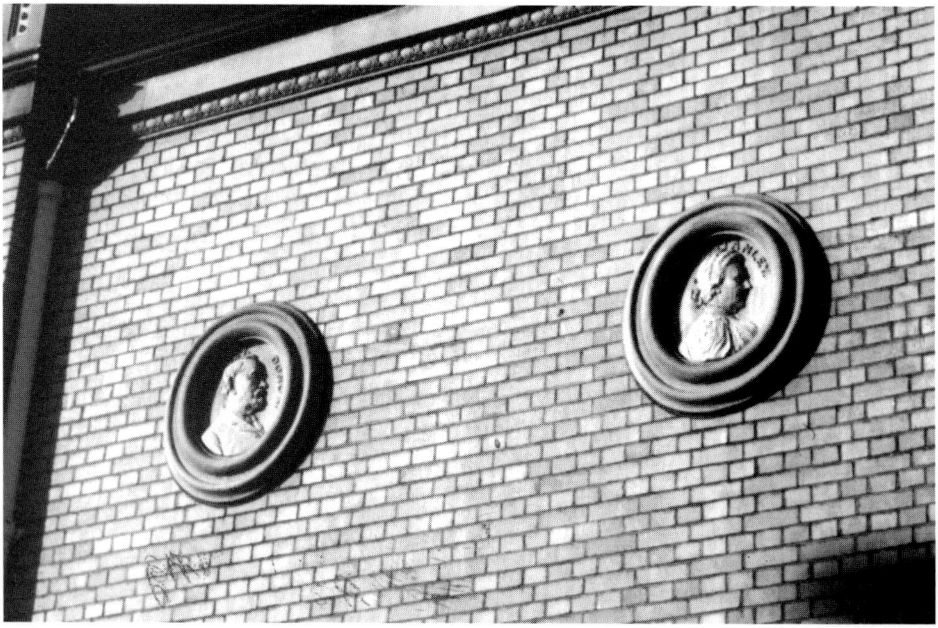

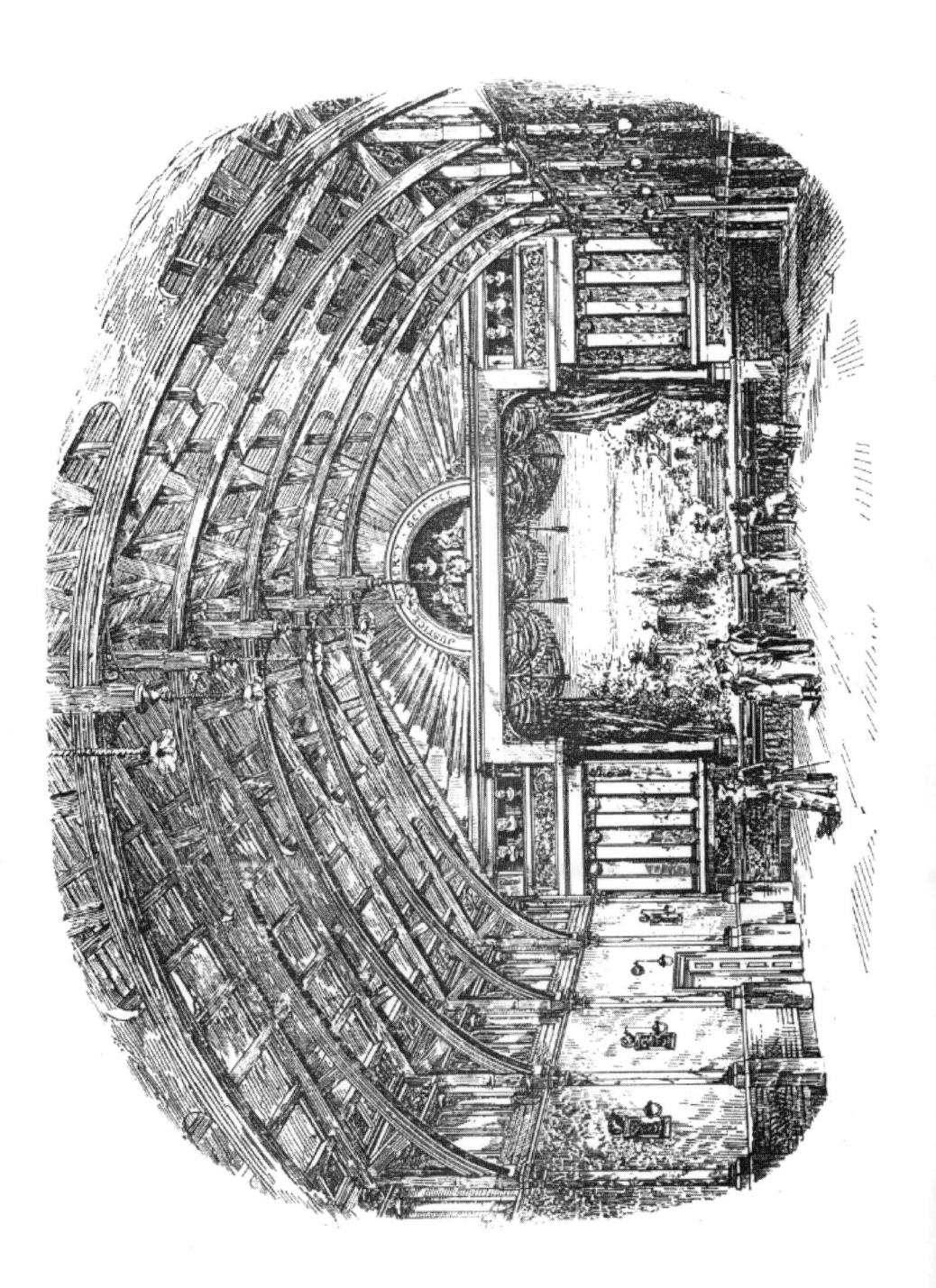

Interior Large Hall

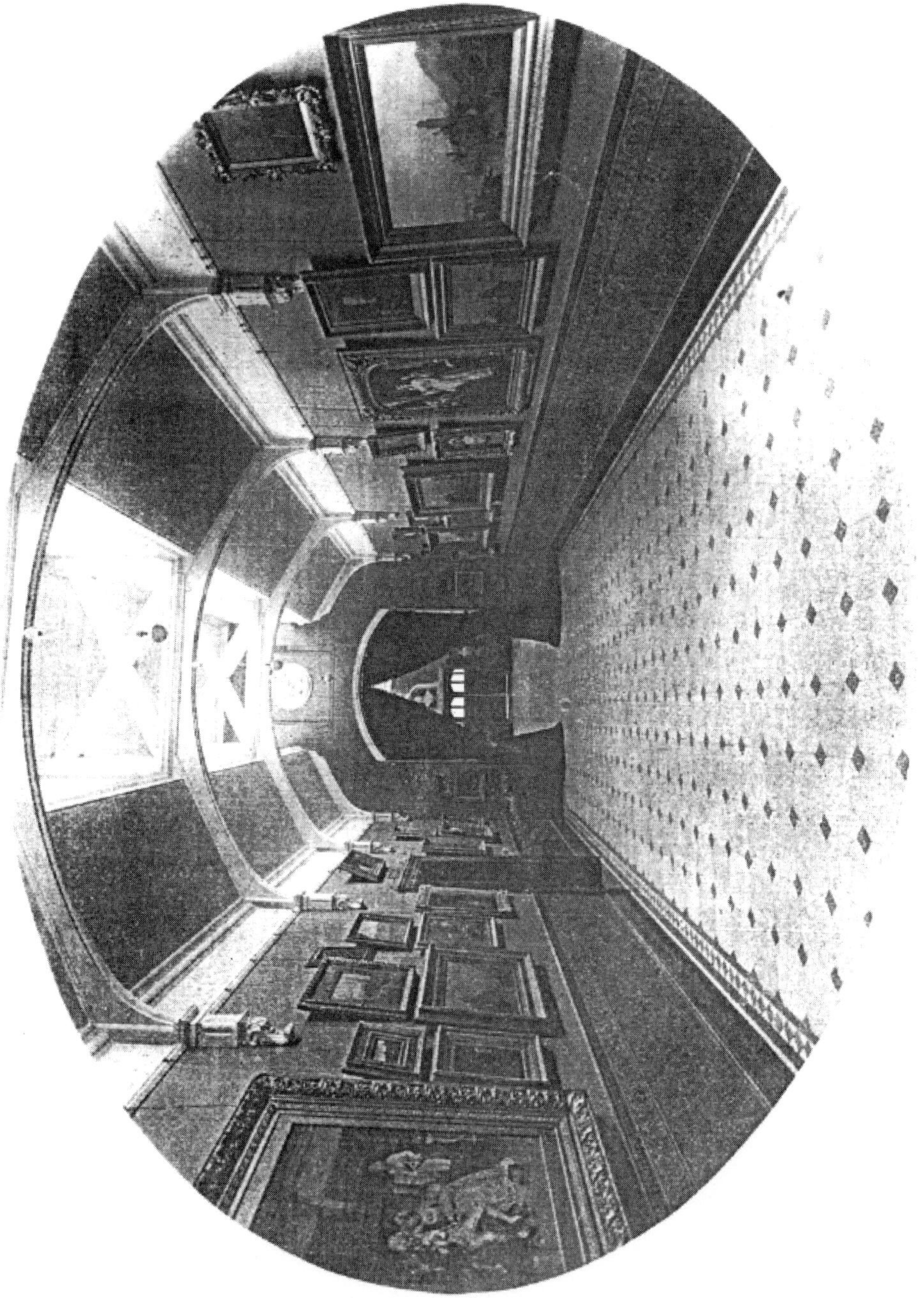

remains, a life-size workman in leather apron wielding a hammer and inscribed LABOR OMNIA VINCIT. Efforts are being made to find funds to replace the busts.

It is a measure of its founder's energy and determination that the Hall was ready for opening early in 1903, the Foundation Stone having been laid by Mrs Stanley in May, 1902. Undaunted by the fact that he was an engineer, not an architect, he nevertheless designed it himself down to the smallest detail - and there are lots of details! The Hall cost him £13,000, according to his own probably rather over-modest calculation, and it provided and provides space for plays, concerts, poetry-readings and lectures and was an instant success. South Norwood's other famous son, the musician Samuel Coleridge-Taylor frequently conducted there. William Hurlstone, another local musician who died very young of the dreaded consumption, composed a song to Stanley's lyric "Eliza" which must certainly have been performed on many occasions. Stanley left a small bequest to Hurlstone's mother in his will.

The following year it was felt that a smaller hall was also required for rehearsals and events involving fewer people. This is a delightful miniature theatre built of the same good quality materials as its bigger sister, and is now used by the School. It also includes a committee room and a kitchen as the need of these had been felt by the users of the big hall. Also responding to popular demand, a clock-tower was incorporated. William Stanley was rather like an indulgent parent to the people of South Norwood, providing them with what they asked for.

Pevsner, in his Buildings of London 2, South, may, perhaps, be said to be damning the buildings with faint praise when he des-

45

cribes them as "the most memorable buildings in South Norwood" and also says that they "... must rank as one of the most eccentric efforts anywhere at a do-it-yourself free style" but he takes the trouble to describe their main architectural features and particularly notes the "extraordinary motif of copper flowers in flowerpots" on the gabled rooflines. These were removed when the buildings were being refurbished in 1987 and not at first replaced, but as a result of the noble efforts of some members of the Croydon Society, and with a grant from the Croydon Preservation Trust, replicas of the original clay pots, which had been broken, were made and the copper flowers reinstated to once more adorn the Norwood skyline. The big hall is still used for performances, dancing classes, aerobics, and also weddings and other functions. More evidence of Stanley's generosity is seen in the dressing-rooms. There are only two, one for each sex, but they are spacious and each has a marble fireplace which would do honour to anybody's living-room.

The Hall is, in the year 2000, lovingly cared for by Zoe Harris on behalf of Croydon Council, aided by George Gage and Dave Evans. George and Dave are both from long-established Norwood families and share an interest in history, because they have memorable relatives. George's great-uncle, most wonderfully named Jawoka Kinkerman Gage in honour of two famous battles of the Crimean War, was on board the first ship sunk at the Battle of Jutland and is the first name on the war memorial in Plymouth and Dave's grandmother was a Pankhurst.

George Gage's grandfather, a bricklayer who helped to build the Hall, must have been one of the 95 workers invited to a great dinner, the first function ever to be held in it on 1st February, 1903, a thank - you from Stanley for all their efforts. After the dinner the wives, mothers, sweethearts and children joined the party for a performance in the theatre in which the whole Stanley family took part, acting, singing and playing musical instruments. The foremen were presented with pocket-rules with their names inscribed on them.

Not content with providing the hall, and himself also designing the friezes of Tragedy and Comedy on each side of the stage, Stanley then set about creating the organisations which would provide the entertainments to take place there, the Stanley Athenaeum, the Norwood Amateur Operatic Society and the Stanley Dramatic Club. The Athenaeum had 600 members and met every Monday evening for talks and discussions. Samuel Coleridge-Taylor conducted a small orchestra at the opening of these occasions. It was still in healthy existence until its tenth season, 1912-1913, when Dr Pinkerton was its President. An elaborate programme was produced that year, the cover decorated with the columns from the side of the stage at the Hall, its substantial size incorporating advertisements from several local firms. None of those in the South Norwood High Street, Craddock the fishmonger, Hillier the draper, Stackell the butcher, Reeves Menswear, Clark the tailor remain. There is still, of course, an Off Licence, but it is not Ellis & Son selling Australian wine at 1/9 per quart! Twenty performances were promised for the season, including seven plays, as well as concerts, lectures and comedy programmes. No further programmes are to be found - presumably the 1914 war brought this, as so much else, to an end.

Next to the Concert Hall an Art Gallery was also built and filled with 70 paintings, gradually added to until there were 144. Naturally, a Stanley Society was soon founded to encourage interest in painting. With his touching faith in the permanence of the established order he had a marble plaque engraved with the words

"OPEN FREE TO THE PUBLIC, WEDNESDAYS MARCH TO OCTOBER 2-5, NOVEMBER TO FEBRUARY 2-4", but in 1959 the collection was dispersed, after thieves had raided it, and the space now houses a small bar. 69 paintings were sold; the remainder, including a water colour by Stanley himself of the gardens of the Crystal Palace, are stored very safely indeed in the former cells under the old Croydon Town Hall, being occasionally brought out for exhibition.

On Monday, 2nd February, 1903, - Stanley's birthday, for he was fond of celebrating that event in spectacular ways - the first Hall was opened with ample pomp and circumstance, by the Rt. Hon. C. T. Ritchie, M.P. He was Chancellor of the Exchequer in A. J. Balfour's Government and Conservative member for the Borough of Croydon at the time. In his opening speech, Stanley said that he was afraid the building might look a little amateurish (cries of No! No!), but that from his examination of buildings in Greece, Rome and Egypt and elsewhere he was convinced that it was built solidly enough to last a thousand years. He did not foresee that in the 1950s and 60s a dementia of demolition would seize the country, but mercifully the Halls were spared that. Nor did he foresee the vandalism of a later decade which would rob the building of some of its exterior decorations, but the structure remains solid and useful, at least after the first hundred years, and it is now Grade II listed.

He was prepared to cover any further expenditure that would be proved to be necessary once the Halls were in operation, and it is interesting to note that he thought a generator might be required to make electricity if that provided by the Electricity Board should prove too costly! Mr Ritchie, in his reply, spoke of the need of Britain to compete with foreign countries and said that if asked what advice he would give to the country in connection with this trade competition he would say "Education, education, education" a phrase used by Tony Blair, Labour candidate for Prime Minister in the 1997 election campaign. It has proved easier, since 1903, to improve the electricity supply than the education system!

The Norwood News and Penge Urban Chronicle of 7th February, 1903 provided an exhaustive description of the ceremony and of the details of the building.

Mr Ritchie, when he spoke of the need for education, had expressed Stanley's own sentiments, so his next task was to build a school. He had long admired the Trade Schools in Germany. He was concerned that boys, in particular, were leaving school at 14 without any foundation for earning their way in the world. With a smattering of the three Rs, many took dead-end jobs, delivering or labouring but were then, at 21, no better equipped to earn a good wage than they had been seven years before. He wrote:

> The average English boy when he leaves school at 14 is left surrounded by mysteries which to him seem quite incomprehensible. He has no knowledge of the heavens above him, nor of the earth beneath his feet, nor of the structure of his own body, nor of any science in the work-a-day world of things around him. All is mystery. Of the construction of the steam engine which conveys him to town, the clock that indicates time, the electricity that produces light, gives power, conveys messages, and of any other common things he is generally quite ignorant. It will be readily seen that if he had continued the kinder-

garten system of education, introducing practical examples of science suitable to his age, he could easily have grafted his intelligent observation on the subjects enumerated above. We find this idea followed in the schools of all the Teutonic races. Upon a boy's general intelligence at about the age of 12 we could further substantially specialize his education on some subjects that would be a particularly useful asset to his prospect of life.

He saw that the lack of a skilled workforce was holding the country back and was distressed by the fact that, when taxis were introduced in London, 2000 Renaults were imported from France, as there was no factory in England able to supply them. He therefore created the Stanley Trades Schools where the boys learnt engineering; they were the first of their kind in England. He was convinced that boys should not be sedentary for too many hours of the day and set up sandwich courses, inspired by what he had seen in Germany, in which they studied at their desks for an hour and a half and then transferred to work benches for practical instruction. He had noticed that technical schools had been set up in France and the result had been a great leap forward in their manufacturing industry. He hoped that the same thing could be achieved in Britain. His meteorometer installed on the roof was to enable the boys to study the weather.

Included in Richard Inwards's book is the text of a paper Stanley wrote on Technical Trade Schools and their purposes and on his own school in particular, in which he gives every detail of the way in which the boys' work should be organised and their days filled.

Before modernisation

After modernisation in 1958

STANLEY TECHNICAL HIGH SCHOOL

was opened on Tuesday, March 26th 1907, and since then, the success of generations of scholars has earned the school a fine reputation for its balanced and relevant curriculum.

The School's founder Mr W F Stanley JP

The school owes much to its founder Mr W F Stanley who was a very successful victorian businessman as well as a noted educationalist and novelist. Many of the concepts found in his novel, "The Case of Theodore Fox...A Political Utopia" were applied to his 'experiment'; a technical and trades school which was designed to produce young trained men to be "coveted as apprentices by our technical manufacturers" and help redress the state of Britain's decaying industries. A concept that is as relevant today

STANLEY TECHNICAL HIGH SCHOOL

has retained the best features of traditional education whilst remaining modern in outlook.

Throughout the years Stanley Technical High School has undergone many changes in order to meet the challenges of the day.

Trade workshops have been re-equipped to provide modern technology workspaces. Extra science laboratories have been added along with computer study rooms and a business study suite.

The school curriculum is further enhanced by extra-school activities such as overseas visits to widen modern language classes and field study courses to bring geography and history lessons to life. In all other areas the school seeks to make instruction as relevant as possible and to allow pupils to experience a wide range of activities that will, in turn, enrich their lives.

Stanley School – today

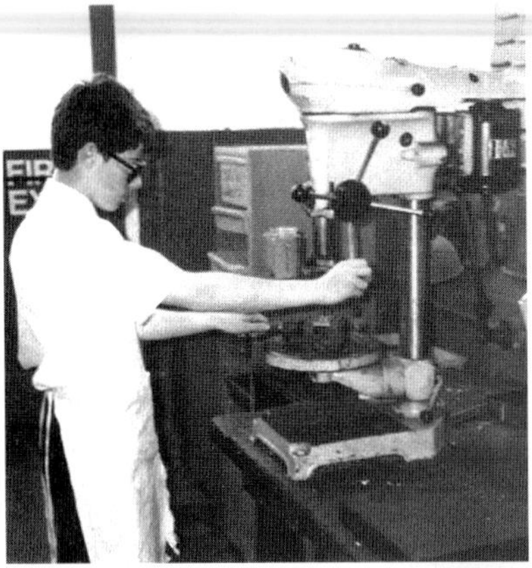

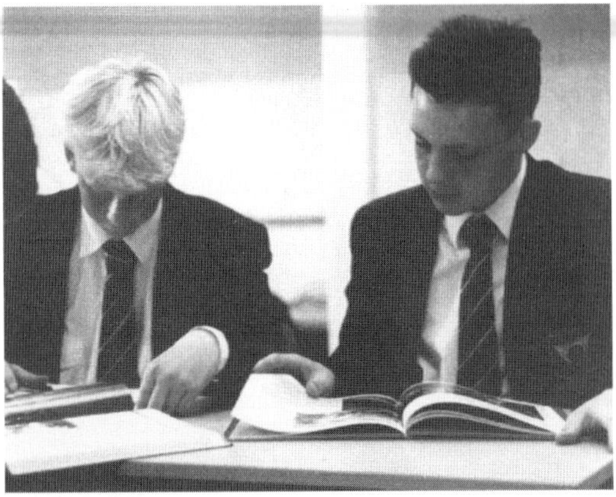

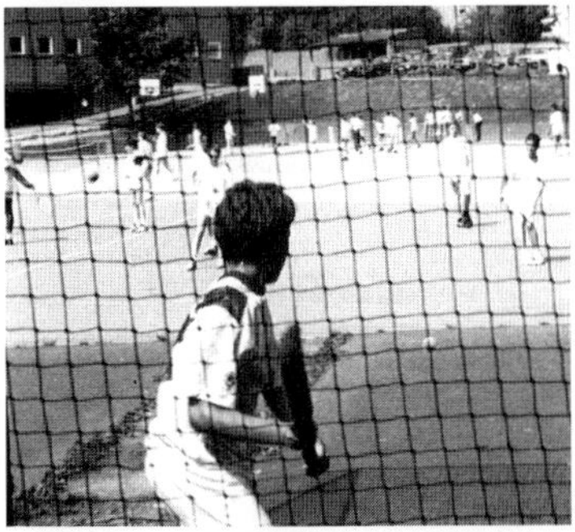

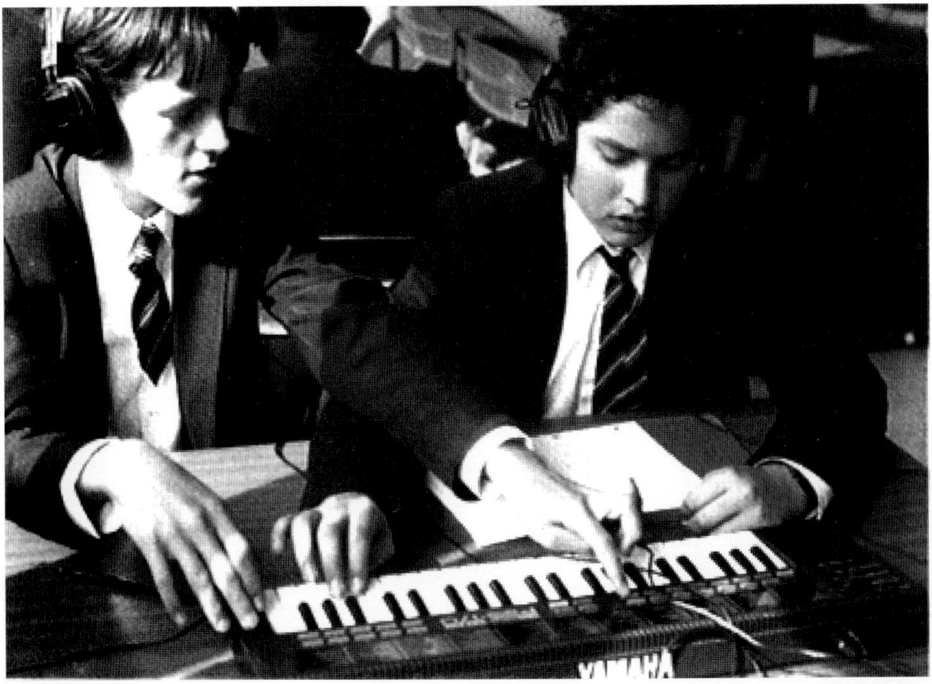
YAMAHA

Also in 1903 Stanley published his prognosis for 1950, under the guise of a novel called "The case of The. Fox", Theodore Fox being the hero who, under hypnosis, foretells the future. In it the channel tunnel, a unified Europe, simplified currency, abolition of the House of Lords, replacement of the monarchy by a republic, but with the Heir to the Throne as President, money replaced by "little plastic cards", X-rays, the banning of fox-hunting are all foretold, but about half a century too soon as he did not predict the two world wars, thinking that the unification of Europe would prevent them. He was also optimistic in thinking that by 1950 public opulence and private simplicity would be the rule and that the real wealth of a country would be seen to lie in the educated intelligence of its population. This book is in the British Library but hard to find elsewhere. Perhaps it could bear reprinting? A longer synopsis can be found in Appendix 2.

The opening of the School was reported in detail in the Croydon Advertiser and Surrey County Reporter of 30th March, 1907. It cost £50,000 to build and was given as a free gift to the public and endowed with £25,000 in freehold properties in the neighbourhood. Fees, were, however, charged, being one shilling a week, but these could be waived if the boy's father was unemployed. Stanley used to give a magic lantern show at the annual Christmas treat, and he contributed prizes for excellence. The school, now Stanley Technical High School still exists today, as a Voluntary Aided Comprehensive Day School for boys aged 11-16. The original complement of 50 pupils has grown to 748. In 1998, 61% of Year 11 went on to further education, 8% to work-based education and 21% to full-time employment. One feature of the 1907 teaching we are perhaps quite glad not to see on the curriculum today is rifle-shooting. War Office pattern rifles were used, ammunition was provided free and the school was a member of the National Rifle Association. Stanley inaugurated the rifle range by firing the first shot himself - he did not, it is reported, hit the bull's eye! A history of the school is being prepared for the celebration of its centenary in 2006.

At the time of his death Stanley was involved in negotiations for the purchase of land at New Eltham for the construction of a factory to produce Navigational Instruments. To this end he had also acquired Heath Navigation, as they had the ability to produce these instruments and Stanley's did not. The required land needed drainage because of the existence of the River Shuttle, behind Sparrows Lane. He gave freely a portion of this land to Avery Hill College, now part of the University of Greenwich, for a sports field to make it unnecessary for them to destroy their gardens for this purpose. There were many delays to this project and Stanley did not live to see even the laying of the foundation stone.

Stanley was also very interested in the Polytechnics which were being created in the 1890s to give further education to those not going to University. One was set up in Thornton Heath and one in South Norwood, the latter being fortunate in having him as Chairman to energetically champion its cause. In 1902 it was enlarged and refurbished, but soon he had to fight, and lost, a battle to save it when, after just a few years, it was decided to have only one in central Croydon. This has now, in its turn, become Croydon College.

On 2nd February, 1907, the Stanleys celebrated their Golden Wedding and William's 78th birthday with a great party at Cumberlow and on the 22nd came the official celebration at the Stanley Hall where the couple were presented with an illuminated address which read:

Watercolour of view from Crystal Palace gardens by William Stanley,
with permission of Croydon Council

The Stanley Clock Tower

Anderman King raising his hat and calling for three cheers for Mr and Mrs Stanley

To Mr and Mrs W.F. Stanley: The inhabitants of South Norwood and its vicinity wish to convey to you their hearty congratulations on the happy event of your golden wedding day, and to express the very high esteem and regard in which you are justly held by them. To commemorate the auspicious occasion they are erecting in the High-street, South Norwood, a clock tower, which will be a lasting testimony to their appreciation of the many benefits you have conferred upon the neighbourhood, and they heartily wish you a continuation of the Divine blessing, with every happiness in the future. On behalf of the committee, F. King (Chairman), J. Roberts (Hon. Treasurer), T. Wickham Jones (Hon. Secretary).

The pretty and useful little clocktower, for which the money was raised by public subscription, is now Grade 2 listed. It is still the focal point of South Norwood, which has become a Conservation Area, so its future should be assured for a good many years to come. On 8th July of the same year Croydon conferred upon him the Freedom of the Borough.

Stanley was still not resting on his laurels, for on January 29th, 1908 he patented an Improved Appliance for Mending Surveyors' Band Chains, nor was he discouraged by the cool reception he had of his ideas about the Cause of Earthquakes and Volcanoes, for he addressed the Stanley Athenaeum on that subject in February.

IX

DEATH

On 2nd August, 1909, the Bank Holiday Monday, Mr and Mrs Stanley were entertaining their adopted daughter, Lilie and her husband, Dr Pinkerton to dinner at Cumberlow, when Stanley felt ill and the doctor encouraged him to go to bed. He had been in poor health for some months, but had been resolutely battling on with his last task, which was a further addition to the Stanley Halls, two committee rooms, still in the same lavish style as the other buildings, with a flat above them intended for the Secretary of the Halls. True to form, next morning Stanley insisted on showing a visitor over the Trade School, and in the next few days his condition worsened. He was desperately keen to see the completion of the addition, but this time his determination was not enough. The specialist who had treated him in his previous illness, Sir Malcolm Mason, was called in and, to Mrs Stanley's joy, thought he might recover, but there was the complication of a kidney failure and in the night of August 13/14th he suffered a heart attack and died at 1.45 in the morning. He was 81 years old.

The funeral took place on Tuesday, 19th August and it was a very grand affair, but also a day of sincerely felt sorrow for the people of South Norwood. The cortege consisted of 15 carriages with 14 filled with family and dignitaries while, in keeping with the way the Stanleys lived, the 15th carried the domestic staff from

FLORAL TRIBUTES TO THE LATE MR. W. F. STANLEY

By permission of the Surrey Evening Echo

The above photograph gives but a faint idea of the immense number of most beautiful wreaths and floral tributes sent by sympathising relatives and friends.

The grave in Elmer's End Cemetery

Cumberlow. It proceeded from the house down Chalfont Road, past the Halls where the flags were at half-mast, and along the High Street where, spontaneously, the householders had pulled their curtains and the shops were closed. The Clock Tower was draped in black crape. The flag over the Town Hall in central Croydon was flown at half-mast. The service was held at St. John's Church, Auckland Road and the vicar, in a fine address said that William Stanley was:

> ... great because of all that he has been able to accomplish in scientific work, not to create marvels, not to terrify mankind, but to turn that great ability he possessed to profit and usefulness, and that which tends to the progress of humanity throughout the civilised world. We think of him as a great philanthropist ... who came forth as a scholar to think how he could work to permanently heal some of the sores of England.

The cortege went at walking pace to Elmers End Cemetery, Beckenham, and was met at the gates by scholars from the Trade School and members of staff from the London and Norwood branches of the firm.

There were obituaries in several distinguished newspapers and journals. The Times wrote, among other things, in several column inches, that he was:

> ... patentee of inventions that had world-wide use ... erected and equipped the Stanley Technical Trade Schools where boys receive general education and technical training combined. As they are largely experimental the progress of these schools is being

closely watched by educationists and the Board of Education has adopted a wholly friendly attitude towards them. They have been endowed with a property valued at £25.000.

The Norwood Herald produced a whole supplement devoted to him and on 21st August had a full-page obituary headed with his portrait and pictures of the funeral cortege. The Norwood News had a five-column obituary, headed "The late Mr W.F. Stanley, J.P., F.G.S., F.R.A.S., F.R.Met.Soc., Educational Optimist, Founder of a famous firm, Designer and Donor of Stanley Halls and Trade Schools, A Notable Norwood Octogenarian". The Engineer wrote:

> Although ... not himself an engineer he has done much for the advancement of the profession ... he was always characterised by ingenuity and indomitable perseverance... the firm acquired a world-wide reputation for satisfactory work. His death, which occurred at his home in South Norwood, will be keenly felt in the district in the progress of which he has always taken an active interest, promoting its welfare by every means in his power.

The Electrical Review said that his name stood out among the scientific instrument makers of the U.K., indeed of the world, and The Electrician wrote in like terms. Engineering wrote "... probably no single man was ever more enthusiastic in perfecting such instruments as he... His ability and energy found many other channels, but it is undoubtedly in connection with drawing and surveying instruments that his name will live among engineers. His circular dividing engine and the logarithm dividing engine do work which, up to the time they were devised, was looked upon as impossible." The Journal of the Geological Society of London, of which he had been a Fellow since 1884, commented on his books on Nebular Theory and the Properties of Fluids and said that he was a "man of great generosity and public spirit."

Alderman King made a statement at the next opening of the Police Court. He said he had known Stanley for 30 years - he was a man who liked to see justice done and tried to do it himself. He also added that to see the Stanleys in their home was simply delightful. Never had he heard a word of discord - his will was hers and hers was his. At the outset of his career Mrs Stanley was his indispensable helpmeet and during the whole of his career she supported and comforted him, and they lived their life as one. To the country Mr Stanley's removal was a loss; to Croydon a great loss, to South Norwood it was irreparable.

William Stanley was buried at Elmers End, in the part of the Cemetery reserved for those who attended St. John's Church, Auckland Road, Upper Norwood. His tomb has a fine portrait carved in stone - one of the few such tombs in the Cemetery. His widow, Bessie lived on, in the flat over the new Committee Rooms, for four more years. When she died, in 1913, her body was placed in the tomb beside her husband.

X

STANLEY'S HERITAGE

The Company continued to expand after William's death under the direction of his brother, Joseph, and of Henry Thomas Tallack, his long-standing colleague. It amalgamated with four others, including George Heath and Company. Stanley had had a long association with George Heath, and it was Mrs Heath who laid the foundation stone of the factory in New Eltham on 25th September, 1915. Although that factory was not in operation until 1916, by which time Stanley had been dead for seven years, to enter it in 1999 was to feel his stamp on the building - wide, solid, well-built doors and door-frames, quality furniture in the offices, and, above all, an elegant oak staircase, which, it is said, he had noticed on a ship which was due to be broken up and rescued to be the centrepiece of his new building, a reminder of the Stanley Hall where he had also used part of a ship.

The Avery Hill Mansion had been bought, in 1882, and lavishly extended in the succeeding decade, by Colonel John Thomas North, another larger-than-life Victorian plutocrat, though in a very different stamp from Stanley. His rise from rags to riches was even faster, as he went out to Chile on a £1 a week job, and returned 20 years later the "Nitrate King", one of the richest men in England. Nitrates were tremendously in demand for artificial fertiliser and extremely profitable. He was a heavy spender and, not liking cold

The factory gates soon to close for the last time

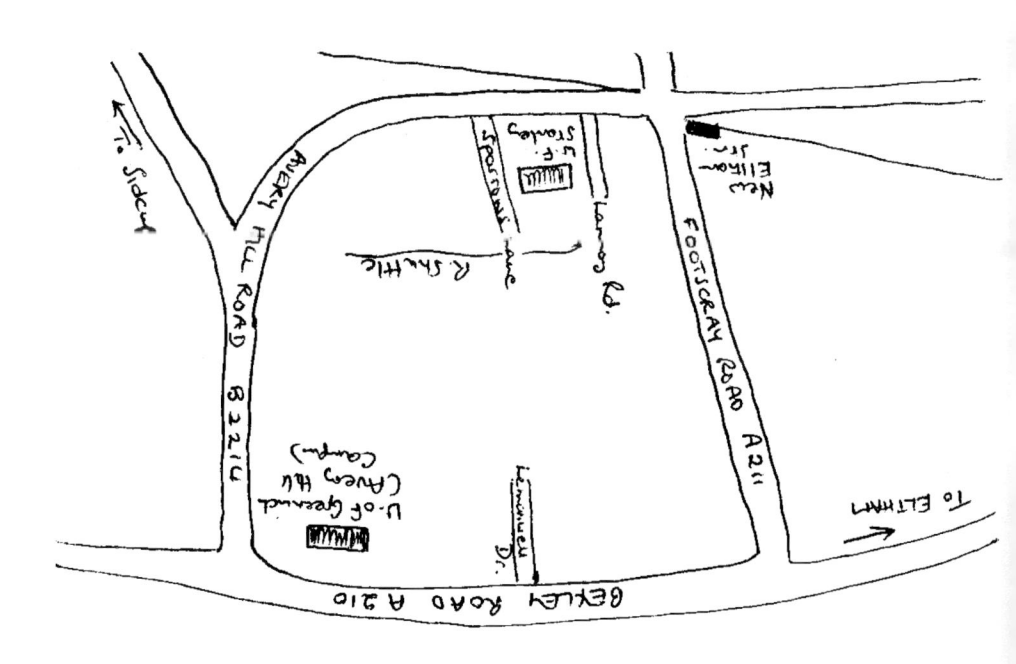

SKETCH MAP AVERY HILL AREA

Colonel North's ballroom, now the College library

Avery Hill College. This picture, dated 1912, shows the main entrance of 1890 to Colonel North's mansion at Avery Hill. Despite air-raid damage in the Second World War, this Victorian feature survives as part of the University of Greenwich

Colonel and Mrs North still welcoming guests to the dining room

Winter garden at Avery Hill

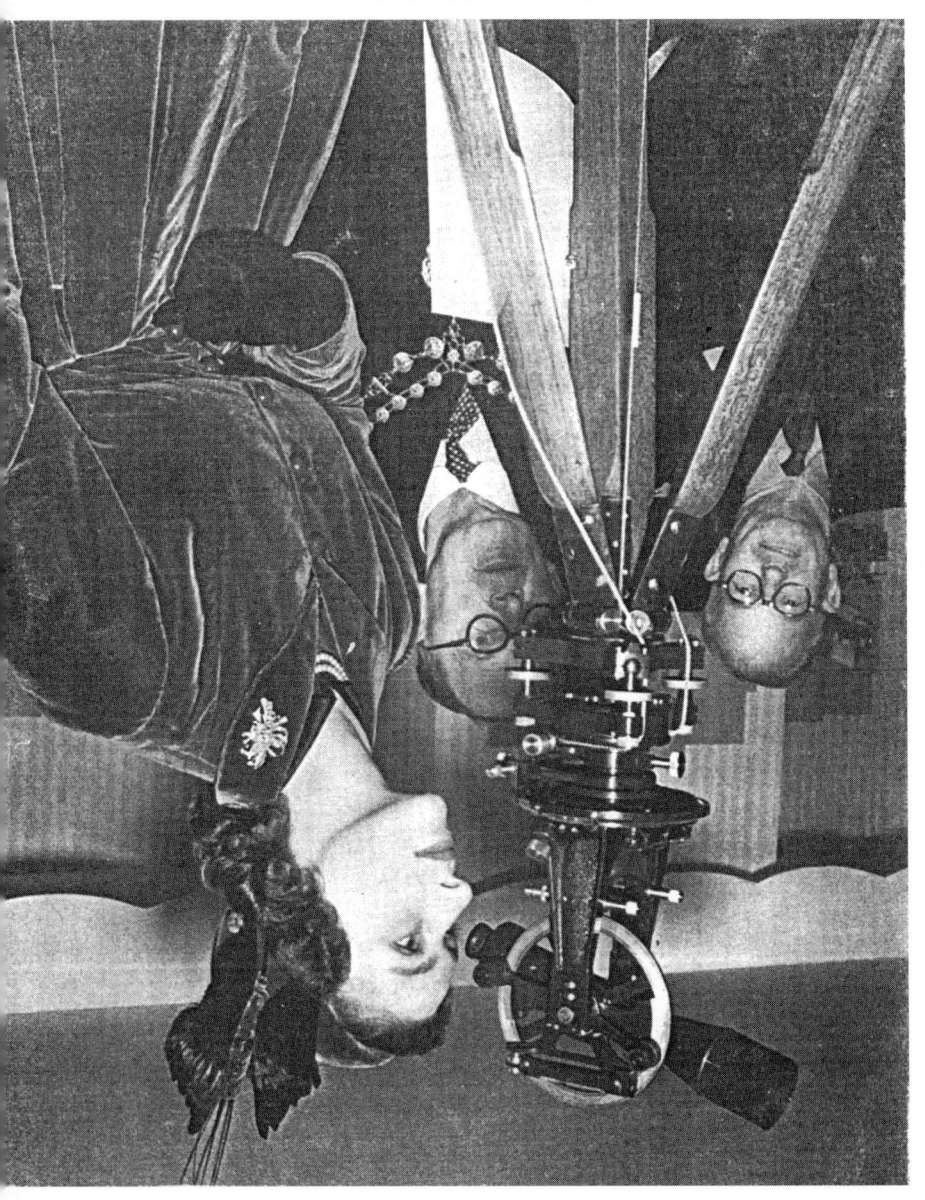

H.R.H. Princess Margaret sighting a Stanley Theodolite at the Borough of Woolwich 'Festival of Britain' celebration on 20th October 1951

By courtesy of Graphic Photo Union

Workshop abandoned 1999

Busy men and machines, 1953

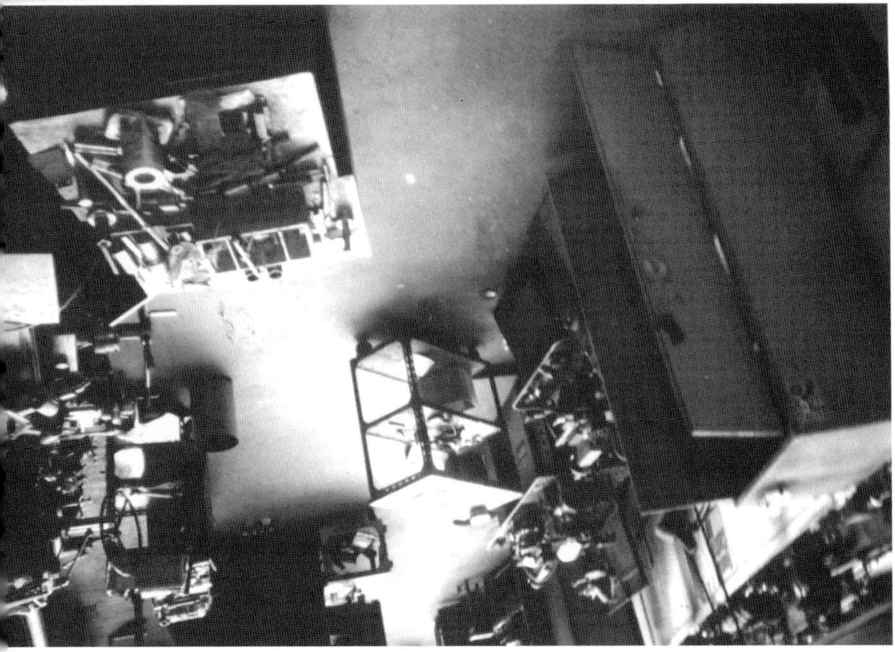

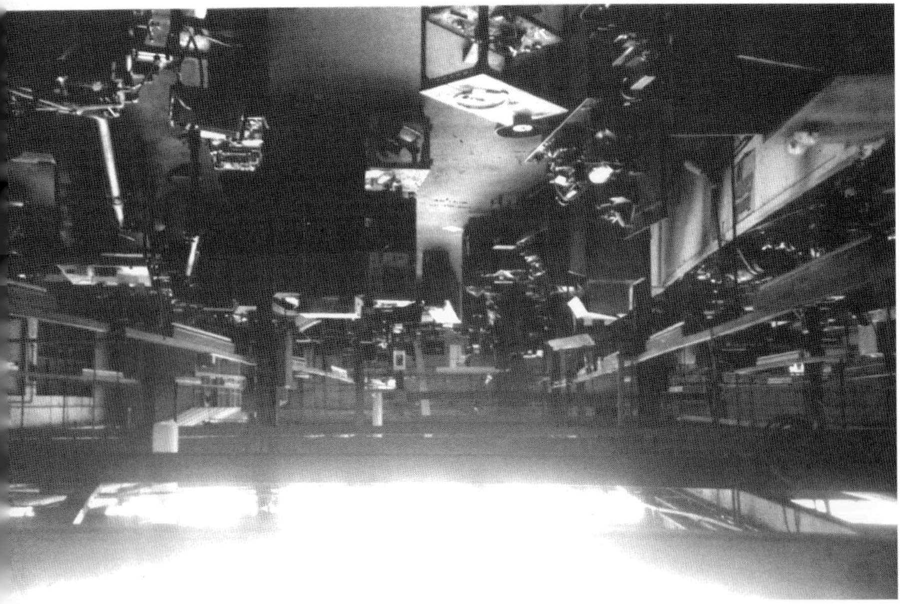

New Bond Street
Clocks and Watches
TUESDAY, 7th DECEMBER 1999

THE CONTENTS OF THE BOARDROOM MUSEUM OF STANLEY INSTRUMENTS

and other related items removed from the Avery Hill Road Works, New Eltham, SE9

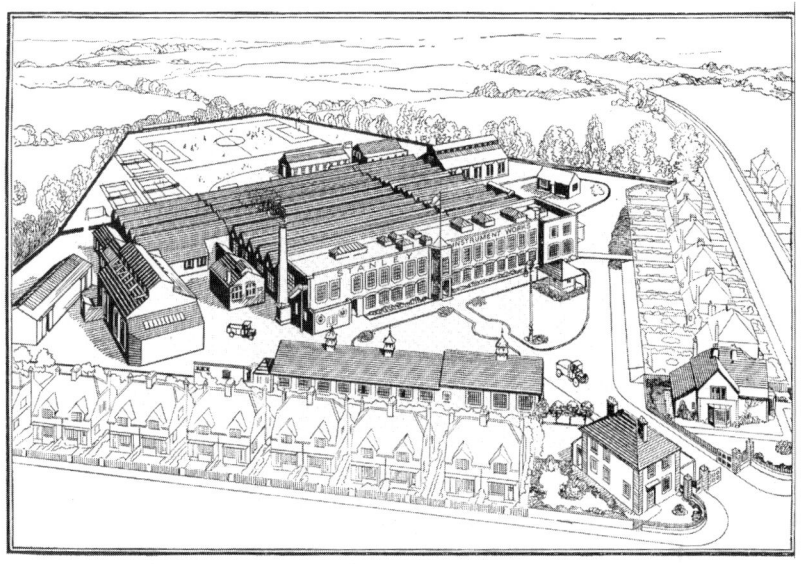

The Stanley Scientific Instrument Works, Avery Hill Road, New Eltham, S.E.9.

By order of the Liquidator A Clarke, of Moore Stephens Booth White

W. F. Stanley & Co Ltd, Mathematical and Navigational Instrument Makers, 1852-1999

W. F. Stanley & Company Ltd was founded by William Ford Stanley in 1853 with capital of £100 at premises in Great Turnstile Street, London, where he made wooden, drawing office instruments, both for sale and for the trade. Stanley's tee-squares, set-squares, parallel rules and curves, being cheaper than the top-of-the-range French equivalents, quickly made an impact on the market.

From the Phillips catalogue, 7th December 1999

Historic instruments ready for sale

winters, but preferring to stay at home, he built an enormous winter garden filled with tropical plants which is still there today. He did not enjoy his home for very long, as he died in May 1896. The family offered it for sale immediately, but it languished, unoccupied, until 1904, when the London County Council acquired it. Much of the house was destroyed by a bomb in World War II but the ballroom still makes a splendid library for the Avery Hill Campus Library of the University of Greenwich and the fine entrance hall is also still intact.

There was enough land left behind the factory for sportsfields for Stanley's own workpeople and on 7th December, 1999 some of the trophies offered for all manner of sports - table-tennis, cribbage, and darts as well as rugby and other out-door sports - came up for sale at Phillips, as part of a Lot which included the beautiful certificates presented to William Stanley on the bestowal of the Freedom of the Borough of Croydon and to Mr and Mrs Stanley on the occasion of their Golden Wedding Anniversary. The author made a bid for this Lot and they will surely find a home on the wall of the school, the halls or the town hall; the cups were bought by Victor Burness, a former second-generation employee of the New Eltham factory, whose father remembered some of the people whose names were inscribed on the cups and shields.

Mr Burness, Senior, is one of many long-time Stanley employees and the story at New Eltham is the same as is reported of South Norwood: everyone around worked at the factory and lived near it, participated in the activities offered, and in some cases three generations of the same family would be working there concurrently. Another former employee, Joseph Merchant, who worked at Stanley's from 1955-1969 still retains a great affection for and collects Stanley instruments and has created a contact point for former employees at Pilots' Pals, the club for flying enthusiasts at Biggin Hill Airport. He regretfully left in 1969 at the time when Smith Industries took over the firm and he realised that there was to be no investment in the new machinery which was required.

There is an amazing story about the survival of the two certificates. A gentleman called Charles Stanley lived in Sevenoaks, no relation to William Stanley, though, by coincidence, he did work at the New Eltham factory. One day, in the 1970s, he was working in his garden when a lady approached him with two scrolls. She said she understood his name was Stanley, that she had found the documents in her attic, and wondered if he would like them. He took them into the factory and handed them to the Managing Director, Alan Mears, who had them framed and hung on the Board Room wall. Thus they came to be included with the instruments and books and catalogues offered for sale at Phillips twenty-five years later. It is likely that the lady who was clearing her attic was either Ada Carey or Maggie Wingfield, two of Joseph Stanley's daughters who lived in Sevenoaks. Since Joseph took on the directorship of the firm when Stanley died, it is probable that he would have inherited his effects, as he was also the only brother living locally.

The factory was requisitioned for uniquely national use as soon as it was completed, before it had actually got into production, but when its capacity was released after hostilities ceased in 1918 it went from strength to strength, spreading its markets and its reputation world-wide. It was requisitioned again in 1939-45, but after that war was over it participated in the huge expansion of airports, tunnels, dams, motorways and housing estates all over the world by supplying quality surveying instruments, notably the theodolite; the Queen Mary and Royal Naval ships used its compasses and other navigational instruments.

In 1953, to celebrate the centenary of the founding of the firm, the Company published a book <u>One Hundred Years of Scientific Instrument Making</u>, by Cecil J. Allen, with the three-fold purpose of paying tribute to their founder, conveying an idea of the part the Company had played in engineering, and inspiring members of the company to greater achievement. At that date the net assets which, in 1853, had been Stanley's £100, were £500,000. F.H.C. Tallack, Henry Thomas's son, was then Managing Director - the tradition of continuity being one of the reasons for the success of the firm. Princess Margaret was present at the celebrations and the photograph of her and others of New Eltham are reproduced from the book.

Three factors contributed to the downfall of the Company and its closure in 1999. First, in an effort to raise money, the site had been sold to a property developer who then leased it back to the factory. They, however, failed to invest the proceeds in the innovative machinery which was beginning to be required. The second factor was the high value of the pound which meant the loss of overseas markets; and the third was dependence on Ministry of Defence orders which dried up after the end of the Cold War. The Company went into liquidation in July 1999. As Allan Mears, the Managing Director from 1975-1999 said "Although the Ministry of Defence was one of our most important customers, we weren't making anything to kill anybody, just things like compasses to help the soldiers and sailors know where they were!"

Stanley had been a Founder Member of The Croydon Microscopical Society, now known as the Croydon Natural History and Scientific Society. In 1949 a new member of the Society, H.W. Dickinson, noticed in the Annual Statement of Accounts, that a substantial contribution to their funds was still coming from shares in the W.F. Stanley company, so he addressed the Society on the subject of their benefactor's life and a photograph was included in the Journal. He concludes:

> He was temperate in all things, strict in his dealings, conscientious and a man of his word, but kindly, considerate and gifted with a sense of humour. He "loved laborious days" and was never content to be idle. He was a born craftsman and a prolific inventor. He was a great believer in self-help - he considered everyone should be the architect of his own fate, as he had been.

It seems worth while to record some of the details of the Will, signed on 20th March, 1908, because it reflects the care Stanley gave to every detail. His wife, of course was well provided for and each nephew and niece, great-nephew and great-niece was mentioned by name and was to receive money and shares. Each servant employed at his home and at the halls and each teacher in the school had £5. Every employee in each factory would receive £2. His brother's wife, Emma received the income from 800 Preference Shares in W.F. Stanley, and his niece, Rose Stanley, 700 shares and "my sweet companion", his adopted daughter, Maud Stanley received 800 shares, but the shares allotted to the family were to carry no voting rights. Small incomes of £1 or £2 a month were left to about a dozen named individuals. Croydon General Hospital received 200 shares,

The 'second-hand' staircase

Alan Mears, last Stanley MD, Stanley Jaeger, Cllr. Ian Croft, Mayor of Croydon, and Jo Stanley on the occasion of the placing of the English Heritage blue plaque, 1993

Salesroom door, to be preserved

as did the Croydon Natural History Society. Croydon Corporation received 100 shares for the purchase of books to be awarded annually as prizes to students in the Croydon Norwood and Thornton Heath Polytechnics and another 100 for prizes in the Council Schools. The British Home and Hospital for Incurables received 100 shares. 200 shares went to the Croydon Police Court Relief Fund, 100 to the Croydon Society for the Protection of Women and Children.

On 8th March, 1993 an English Heritage blue plaque was attached to the wall of the Stanley Halls and unveiled by the Mayor of Croydon, Councillor Ian Croft. It reads:

> William Ford Stanley - 1829-1909
> Inventor, manufacturer and philanthropist
> Funded and designed these Halls
> and Technical School

Jo (nicknamed Dodo) Stanley, a grand-daughter of his brother Edward, came to Croydon from Dorset for the unveiling ceremony, though she was ninety years old. Aged 97, in 2000 she was still living on her own in Bridport, quite sound in mind and body. She was a secretary by profession, and held the certainly very demanding position of Personal Assistant to Lord Reith while he was Director-General of the B.B.C., remaining a friend after her term of employment ended. She remembers at the age of five sitting on William Stanley's knee, and that he always kept sweets for children in a special corner of his desk where they knew they would be always sure to find them, but she did not spend much time at Cumberlow as she and her parents lived in Peterborough. Her father, a second Edward, son of William's brother Edward, moved there to escape William Stanley's powerful personality. He did not want to work in the family firm but valued his independence. He had his own engineering works in Peterborough and was also an inventor and very successful. Jo remembers driving down to London in 1908 in what would have been one of the very early private cars. Her niece, Anne Richardson, lives near Ludlow and visits frequently.

The Stanleys are a strangely unprolific family, and there has been a preponderance of girls, so that, from William's parents, John and Selina's family of nine children, there are only twenty-two in the current generation of youngsters and only one survivor, Josephine (Dodo) with the name Stanley. This trend started because, of the nine, only two produced children. As has been seen, William had no children. Joseph had five girls, one of them, Ethel, continuing the family name by marrying her first cousin, Edward's son, Edward John Stanley. Edward I had two boys and three girls, but of the two boys, John's children did not marry and Edward II's son, Clifford had only girls. Those two girls have many children and grandchildren, but not of the name of Stanley, though they are proud of the connection. It is striking in this family, as in William's case, perhaps for the lack of direct descendants, how the aunt/uncle-nephew/niece relationship has been important in each generation.

Anne Richardson, Edward II's grand-daughter, has four children, of whom one, Kim Moss, has inherited the family genius for invention. He lives in Queensland, Australia, and has invented a special net to keep swimmers safe from the dangerous jelly-fish with lethal sting which haunt those waters. The net is treated with a repellant which, as well as keeping the stingers at bay, prevents it from accumulating all the marine plants and other rubbish which would collect on an untreated net. He also designed the machinery which lets it out into the water and hauls it in. These nets find a

Stanley still remembered on South Norwood High Street

An example of Stanley's cabinet-making skills

Inventiveness continues. Kim Moss's protective nets

ready market and he lives on the income from their sale. He is working on a way of making it possible to drive small boats up the beach and out of the water using their own power.

Stanley Jaeger, Maud's son was also present at the English Heritage ceremony, but he died in 1999. His sister, Elizabeth, now also lives in Bridport, amid many mementos from Cumberlow, including the remarkable piece of furniture pictured here which was carved by William Stanley - in his spare time!

The South Norwood factory, by then a timber works, owned by John Smith of JSM Joinery but still popularly called The Stanley Works, was partially destroyed by fire at the end of 1998. Application has been made to convert it into flats, with preservation of some of the original features, which is required because it is now in a conservation area. Work has started as there is scaffolding up and it appears that the imposing door of the office is to be kept. It is hoped that the building will have a name which will carry some reference to its past and also that a place will be found for the marble plaque over the door.

In 1999 Wetherspoons, conscious, as they usually try to be, of local history, opened The William Stanley, a large public house in 19th Century style on the High Street. A portrait of its namesake has pride of place inside, and there are also pictures of four other Norwood notables, Lily Langtry, H. Tinsley, another scientific instrument manufacturer, Coleridge-Taylor and Brock of fireworks fame.

Further searching of the Internet for confirmation that Stanley is not forgotten yielded evidence of this. A firm called Stanley London, in Anaheim, California, produces small, brass, very detailed and highly polished reproductions of many of Stanley's scientific instruments for decorative purposes, made in India. They write:

> Stanley London is pleased to offer fine brass reproductions of antique sextants, compasses, telescopes, and other surveying and nautical items. These are hand crafted using solid brass and German silver, and are highly polished to a beautiful finish. Most products are stamped "Stanley London", after W.F. Stanley & Co. in London, who made precision instruments one hundred years ago. Many items are available with beautiful handcrafted display and storage boxes. All of these items add sophisticated warmth to an office, and make great gifts for loved ones, collectors and corporate executives.

However, it must also must be mentioned that, as well as these "executive toys" they make replica, full-size instruments which are, unfortunately, sometimes mistaken for the real thing by the unwary when they are resold.

On 7th December, 1999, 36 lots of instruments and records from the factory at New Eltham were auctioned at Phillips. Most of these were bought by collectors, but the Science Museum acquired Lots 25 and 31. These were Deed Boxes, No. 25 containing production and sales ledgers for various individual instruments dated between 1879 and 1984, workshop notebooks and a box file containing correspondence relating to trade with India and a brass box of balance sheets. No.31 contained agreements, trust deeds and leases as mentioned above.

Conclusion

Stanley had no formal religious or political affiliations, just his own strict moral code that he lived by. Perhaps that is the reason that he received no national appreciation of his work in the form of a decoration or knighthood, though it would appear that he had done ample scientific and philanthropic work to merit one. There seem to have been no skeletons in his cupboard. His intellectual and cultural interests and his industry more than account for every moment of his time. In all likelihood, Mrs Stanley, if questioned, would say that her husband's principal vice was his obsessive, and probably most uncomfortable, urge to improve everything in sight. William Stanley can be said to be a public benefactor of the stamp of John Whitgift whose contributions to Croydon made in the 16th Century are still keeping his memory green.

Appendix 1: Some Inventions

Many of the patents applied for were simply improvements on previous ones, so it would be tedious to list them all. Those already mentioned in the text have not been listed.

1868 A simplified machine for creating frictional electricity.
1870 An improved drawing board strengthened by metal bolts and nuts.
1872 An improved method of constructing portable galvanic batteries.
1874 An improved circular saw bench.
1874 An improvement in compass points.
1875 Pendulums for equalizing pressure and temperature and calculating time.
1880 Apparatus for Measuring Distances by Triangulation.
1880 Improvements in the lens-mounting, the dark slide, body of cameras, and focusing.
1883 Integrating Anemometer. Described in the Quarterly Journal of the Royal Meteorological Society.
1885 New Protractor. One of these was sold at Sotheby's on 9th November, 1999 for £150.
1885 Actinometer.
1885 Improvements in buffers to lessen the effect of collision on land and sea.
1885 Barometer and snow-gauge. These devices were exhibited at the Royal Meteorological Society.
1886 Improvements in Chandeliers and Pendants. A contrivance by which the pulleys, chains and balance weights used in raising and lowering the lamps were concealed from.

THE LATEST "HAT"-ROCITY IN AU-TOP-HATIC MACHINES.

"'Sh all righsh, ol' felsh. Don' go slepsh. Push knob; slidsh oom'n' down, y'see!"   "There! wharrer tell ye? Itsh come down!"

Stanley's invention mocked in 'Scraps', 8th December 1888

From the Yorkshire Evening Post, 6th September 1890

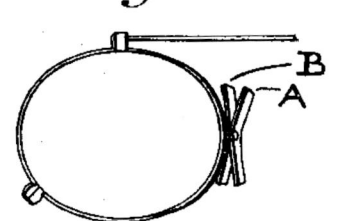

A.D. 1902. Sep. 11. N° 19,909.
STANLEY'S COMPLETE SPECIFICATION.

(1 SHEET)

Fig. 1.

Fig. 1.ᵃ

Fig. 2.

Fig. 3.

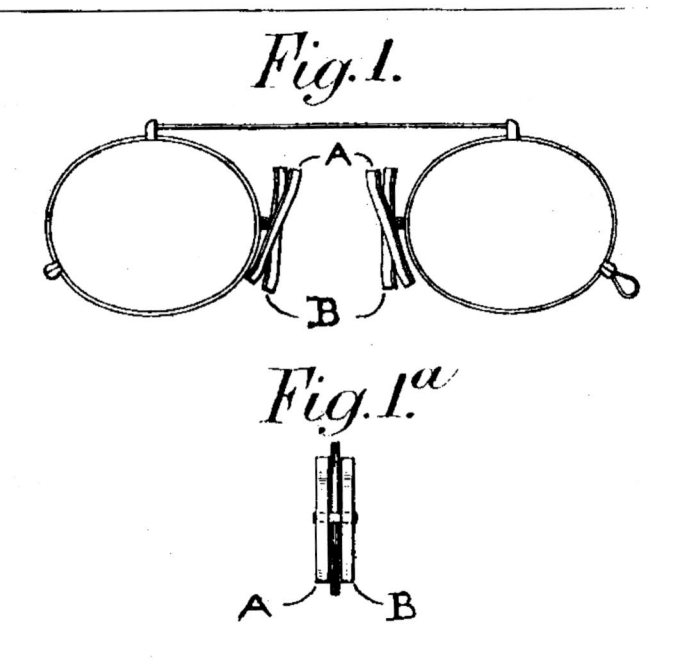

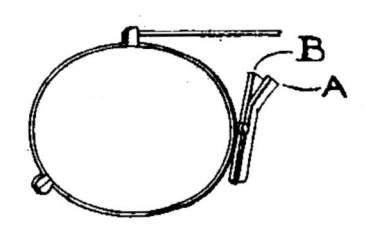

Fig. 2.ᵃ

Fig. 3.ᵃ

1886   An improved carving knife, with which was included a sort of shear for severing the small bones and joints of poultry.

1886   Press for rendering steaks tender.

1886   Copper skewers for conducting heat through flesh and achieving quicker cooking of meat. In the following year, Queen Victoria's Golden Jubilee, these were used in Eastbourne and other places to help in the roasting of whole oxen.

1886   Machine for measuring the height of human beings automatically. One of the first penny-in-the-slot machines, though Stanley took the idea from Alexandria where, in the first century A.D. a few drops of holy water were delivered in response to a coin being placed in a slit in the upper part of the device. (In a letter to Nature in the following year Stanley reports that the average height of Egyptian Mummies was, for males, 5ft.1 ins. and for females, 4ft.7ins. Cleopatra measured 4ft.6ins.)

1886   Design for a saw which could cut down the largest trees but was so portable it could easily be carried in a saddle-bag or even in the pocket.

1887   A Wheel Pen and Spectacles.

1887   A Spirometer - a device for measuring lung capacity, which must have been the predecessor of the peak flow charts so familiar to asthma sufferers today. An illustrated description appeared in the Lancet of February 1st, 1890 and it was patented. It was also one of the ideas presented at a British Association meeting in Leeds in September, 1890, and the Lancet had an article about it, but the Yorkshire Evening Post took a rather more light-hearted view.

1887   Hollow cones inserted into the bases of cooking utensils, which allowed the heat to quickly reach the centre of the vessel.

1888	Stanley's Patent Pen Extractor.
1888	Stanley's Patent Conducting Cake-tin.
1889	Improvements in mining stadiometers, theodolites and tacheometers. One of Stanley's theodolites was presented to the Maritime Museum in Liverpool in 1979 by the Liverpool Dock and Harbour Company and can be seen in the Maritime section of the new museum.
1889	Improved lemon squeezer for use in bars. A lever passed through the bar or table and was operated by one pressure of the foot. This was an extension of the familiar, kitchen lemon-squeezer which probably pre-dates Stanley by many a long year.
1890	A device by which distances could be measured by the time sound takes to travel and was applied to rifles and artillery.
1892	Improvements in Tribrach Arrangements for Instruments of Precision.
1894	Improvements in Planimeters. This device, which enables the area of irregular surfaces to be measured, was originally invented by a Mr Amsler, but Stanley refined it and when the Stanley factory in New Eltham produced its last catalogue in the 1990s the very latest in planimeters was illustrated on its cover.
1895	Improvements in Surveyors' Levels. This was for a level that also measured gradients.
1898	Improvements in mining surveying instruments, including a device for taking sights vertically downwards, such as that down a shaft.
1898	Improvements in Drawing Boards and Tee-Squares. This was for an accurate steel edge to the board and square. Stanley never rested on his laurels, but liked to make further refinements to his own previous patents.

1899 Machine for cutting Brazilian quartz lenses for spectacles.
1900 Improvements in Rotary Engines.
1901 Improvements in Surveyors' Levels. This was for casting the tube and vertical axis in one piece. Stanley's Levels became standard equipment.
1902 Improvement in Self-Holding Double Eye-glasses.
1902 Improvement for Fixing Stone Skirtings to the walls of Buildings. This method was used in parts of the Stanley Technical School buildings and the skirtings are still visible, though not very photogenic.
1903 Improvements in Gauges and Rods for Standard Measures. This was a device for taking exact inside and outside measures by the same gauge.

Appendix 2: Travel

Letters to the Norwood News 2nd March to 25th May, 1889. (In Mr. Inwards's book the name of the ship is given as the "Ceylon", but the letters in the newspaper state that the ship was called the "Jaffa", so it must be assumed that the latter is correct.)

On Cape St Vincent is built a lighthouse and a convent in one building. A solitary rock, yet all the windows are grilled over with iron bars. Is it for fear of intruders from without or wily fisherman that would climb the heights for a better peep at the beauty within, or is it that the naughty nuns will peep out into our wicked world where all is silence, who shall guess?

Gibraltar (of the gardens) Nowhere in my life have I seen Nature and Art combined in such picturesque grandeur. ... a very large percentage of travellers will spend their time in the shops. You may buy here the excellent articles made in Manchester, Coventry and Birmingham, especially for the colonial trade, that you will not see anywhere in England. In so doing, you will show, quite unwittingly no doubt, your appreciation of the taste of our manufacturers, and support our dear old country. You may buy also Eastern articles, but on this point I would advise you to reserve your purchases until you get home, as you may buy better articles and at cheaper price, but of the same description, in many of our Eastern shops in London, and at the seaside resorts.

Tangier ... A perfect *scène de ballet*. The active and stately Moors are treading their stately ways just as in the City of London, but here the colour marks the way of each citizen. It is the Sabbath and many are dressed in long white robes, many in various tints and colours. In a group of three, one is violet, one sandy and one pale orange which seemed to blend charmingly with the Moorish arch behind. Above the motley crowd, figures arise which appear in the distance as giants. These are the stately Moors on stateless donkeys. The cloak nearly covers the little animal which makes it look at a distance like a divided skirt, whereas at a backward view the giant appears to be standing on a four-legged table, the donkey being quite lost except his legs.... This seems to me a place *par excellence* for the artist.... In the market we bought the mature oranges, sold on their long green stalks, which were very different in size and colour and of superior flavour to the article we are told are Tangerine oranges. All kinds of food are sold in the market. We were told we should find the place very dirty. It was not so if compared with a French, Italian or Irish town of the same size. The prison is one of the sights for visitors. Here ten poor fellows are seated in rooms, chained together right foot to left foot through the row of eight or ten. They are kept busy plaiting mats or making very tasty baskets. Their relations, friends, or perhaps scoffers can speak to them or joke with them from the gratings so that the wife and child may not be entirely lonely or lost for the sins her husband suffers, as with us, but whether we are the more humane on the whole with our silent system I am not able to judge.

Malta The grand harbour is very charming. It is divided into five creeks, four of which spread out rather like the fingers of a hand... At present there are three ironclads in the harbour and the Duke of Edinburgh is here. These ships are visited by invitation. The Alexandra is the flagship but the Benbow is the principal attraction as she carries two 110-ton guns, which throw shots, costing £500 each, to a distance of 14 miles, it is said. We attended Divine Service on the Duke of Edinburgh's ironclad. The pulpit was erected on the mouths of two large guns, a curious position for preaching the doctrine of peace from which the reader may draw a moral.... One of the sights the visitor is led into is the Franciscan monastery, where the good monks are not buried, but after death are set up in standing positions in niches in the walls until they become skeletons. An oak bar is placed across the chest, upon which the arms are supported, and the heads and hands are placed in various fantastic positions. They are in full dress. The living monks look very dirty and sorrowful, as though they are always contemplating the fantastical position in which they may in future be placed. ... A list of sacred relics is suspended on the wall of St John's - a thorn of Christ's crown, a fragment of the sacred cradle in which Jesus lay, a stone with which St Stephen was stoned, the right foot of Lazarus, and they have some pieces of the True Cross.... No doubt these things form a great source of happiness.

Alexandria A very short stay here is quite sufficient for the sightseer. The celebrated Cleopatra's needle is now properly fixed on the Thames embankment and will no doubt soon be forgotten by Londoners. The fellow needle has been taken down and sent to America, where, it is presumed, its beauty will be appreciated. Pompey's pillar remains, but this is a poor affair - not worth putting on the official screw to get the Khedive's permission to take it.

Cairo ... The primary education is very interesting. There are over 1000 boys of ages from 5 to 9 in one school under a colonnade, packed together very closely. The master sits in the centre of a circle of little ones, who are in the most part engaged in writing dictation. The children are perfectly quiet and keep constantly to their work. Children at 7 write Arabic with great clearness. Possibly some of our very economical School Boards could get a hint here. A small sheet of tin plates takes the place of a slate, and upon this pen and ink writing seems very easy. The ink is a sort of cake blacking to which water is added as required. The smooth surface of the plate wears out very few pens. Any child who does not learn his lesson or do his work is consigned to a public whipping-master... this part of the affair is most brutal and makes one dubious of the efficiency of the general education.

Jerusalem ... Against the temple walls the Jews meet for public wailing on the eve of the Sabbath. Here they have wept with little intermission for 1800 years for the restoration of the temple. Whether their wailings will avail will depend, I presume, very much on the Jews themselves. They have now wealth and influence with the Courts of the world, and are able to put on the diplomatic screws, but the modern Jew does not stand quite still in passing time and generally looks upon his brethren now more nearly as a national society than as a religious state. ... I cannot close without mentioning the tombs of the kings, excavated at the beginning of the century by some learned Frenchmen ... What is particularly interesting is the rolling stone by which they are closed ... it is like a wheel, or, more precisely, a grindstone. It rolls sideways from the entrance in a groove, so that when it is closed it fits flat like a door and perfectly closed the entrance.

Constantinople Arriving on a Friday we went to see the Sultan go to his mosque ... This little Friday journey is said to be all that is seen of the Sultan in public. The arrangements for his protection are very clever. Visitors can see him only when they are standing up in carriages. The carriages are placed down a slope and there are five lines of cavalry placed in front of them. The head of the Sultan becomes just visible between the heads of the soldiers. Foreigners only go to see him. The natives are not fond of him. It is said they have no reason to be. He appears very pale and has an anxious, suspicious look. As he passes, the soldiers, upon signal, cheer him. I suppose this takes the place of the cheers of the people. A splendid baritone voice from the top of a minaret calls to prayer with a fine musical chant.... The celebrated bazaars are full of merchandise from all countries and I was pleased to see our own country well represented.

Corfu was in holiday attire when we arrived on 6th April, the anniversary of the Greek independence of the Ionian Isles. The people appeared a little sorrowful and there was no display of flags or any other mark of festivity, except at the hotels. We had a native guide to show us the city, and I remarked that the city did not look very jubilant for such an occasion. He said they had found out they had made a mistake in asking for independence. They were very prosperous with plenty of trade and little taxation under the English rule, but at present they were heavily taxed, with little trade from the loss of the English money that used to pour into the place. The general appearance verified this. The roads were getting out of repair and there was the want of the general civic order which English government always secures. ... Upon the quay are many barrels of good red wine, which, we are informed, will be sent to France, to be reshipped at three times the cost, for French claret.... One matter has impressed me constantly in my travels, which their wine reminds me of, as this wine will probably eventually reach our country ... that it would be of great value to our commerce if we require the stately English Consul, of good family and of education limited only to college life, to have also a deputy "man of the world sort of fellow" who had some education in commerce, to set certain lines of trade moving which could ultimately work some good to poor John Bull's pocket.

Messina Arriving at this place on Italian soil one appears to lose all touch of Eastern life... The dresses have now become London dresses and the shops London shops. The local business appears to be pickled lemons and oranges of which the quays are full of casks. This, I am told, is the first process in the manufacture of candied peel for our Christmas puddings.

Palermo A great many English people are here and it is said to be a very fashionable winter resort for those fond of city life.

Naples I return to Naples seventeen years from my first visit. Behold the change! Seventeen years ago the beautifully bright blue Bay of Naples sparkled in the sun. Fishermen's huts studded the shore, the brightly coloured fishermen's boats were drawn up on the beach with picturesquely-dressed natives standing near them ... In the city there was only one decent street with filthy alleys leading thereto, exhaling a pestilential odour from amidst a people clothed in rags ... Today all is changed. The bay is slightly muddy with sewage. The fishers' huts have disappeared with all the gay colours and clothing. A good, modern quay surrounds the shore, merchants' stores and villas in part extend to the water's edge. In the city, wide streets with good buildings are opened out or are in course of construction. The city is drained and passably sweet. The people are clothed in modern European dress and appear to be all busy at work. Seventeen years ago the churches were empty and the Pope was cursing the King... All that has changed now. Schools are everywhere and education is compulsory and perfectly free. The good Catholic people, driven from their churches, are there again ... Political suffrage is now universal to all men who now take practical interest in public affairs ... there appears to be no extremes of necessity as evident formerly. Since Victor-Emmanuel's reign no antiquities have been allowed to be taken from the country ... antiquarian research has been carried out with vigour.

I cannot close this letter without a brief note upon Vesuvius, which I ascended ... with mules and guides. It may be interesting to my neighbours to know that I have a theory of the cause of eruptions of volcanoes, on which I read a paper before the Geological Association of London about 15 years ago. ... The associates did not like it and printed only an abstract. My theory is that the accumulation of snow at the North and South poles of the earth by the amount of annual precipitation causes a pressure upon the heated fluid of the interior of the earth and thereby causes eruptions, earthquakes and other phenomena. The beauty of the theory is that I have found no one to believe in it but myself. By this advertisement I invite my dear neighbours to become disciples. If I gain one (?) I will tell my scientific friends of it. If I am told afterwards "But your disciple is not a scientific man" I will reply that the first disciples of new theories are generally poor.

<u>Malaga</u> Being here on Easter Sunday we attended Mass in the cathedral, a large ornamental building of poor taste. The music was very grand. There are in this cathedral two very fine organs, one on each side. These were being played with a full band of stringed instruments. There is, to me, a peculiar charm to stringed instruments with organ accompaniment. Anyone who has heard the fine Sunday morning service at St Roche in Paris will recognise this effect. There was also a full choir with good professional tenor, baritone and bass... in part of the music one organ answers the other, the effect of which is very grand. I was a little astonished at the worship ... At certain parts of the service the verger struck the floor and everyone had to kneel. I did not quite understand this, but a loud tap on the floor

close to my back, with the verger pointing to the floor, brought me down. The priests have legal power in this matter. I remember being at Vienna when [foot] passengers had to kneel even in the muddy streets when the Host was carried along, but I thought this compulsory power of the Church had generally passed away in Catholic Europe.... The poor children in the town appear to be playing about in the streets all day long, or begging of passers-by, just as they were in England twenty-five years ago. I recollect that at about this time the Society of Arts published a map of Europe showing the state of education in different countries by means of light and shade. In the map England and Spain were in the darkest parts. I fancy this map much influenced our Education Acts. A map of this kind would be of interest now that we are a shade lighter in the educational scale than Spain, although much behind Europe generally, to the great loss, as it seems to me, of our trade influence abroad. The railroad from Malaga to Granada (ten hours) passes through the very rich valley of Andalusia and over a grand pass of the Sierra Nevada ... the views are so charming as to rivet the attention of the traveller the whole way.

Granada It was a new chapter of English history to see the cloister leading to the monastic church lined with paintings in which Oliver Cromwell was a leading character in scenes not given in our histories. One picture represented him having twenty priests shut up and starved to death ... another .. a large chaldron with a fire under it, set up in a public street in the City of London, before which Cromwell was not only having priests cut up alive and boiled but women and children as well... Referring to our guide as to his belief in these thing he said they were quite true and seemed astonished I did not know of it. This ... makes me think better of the Spanish people of the Inquisition period.

The Alhambra I obtained my impressions of the Alhambra from the court at the Crystal Palace and had concluded that the true Alhambra was a small, elegantly furnished palace, of which some of the apartments were reproduced in the Crystal Palace and therefore I was at first astonished to see the Alhambra Palace covered an area almost as large as the whole Crystal Palace - the Court of Lions is at least 100 feet long and completely different, but the fountain of the lions, the most tasteless feature, as I think, of the whole Alhambra, and a part very doubtful of being Moorish work at all as the Muslims never represent living things .. I find is reproduced full size. We have, in the Crystal Palace, a sketch of certain parts of the Alhambra and one small room ... I have walked through the Alhambra of Granada - I have not seen it ... What is a day or two to observe or understand the lifework of many true artists, inspired by deep and devout religious thought, as our medieval artists were. I hope to return one day to study and understand it better.

Appendix 3: Publications

A Descriptive Treatise on Mathematical Drawing Instruments, Their Construction, Uses, Qualities and Suggestions for Improvement; with Hints upon Drawing and Colouring, 1866

When the 6th edition appeared in 1888, English Mechanic commented "... the work remains the best in its class as well as the only original work of its kind. The 7th edition, 1900 was reviewed in Revista de Obras Publicas (Spanish Public Works Review)

Proposition for a New Reform Bill to Fairly Represent the Interests of the People, Simpkin, Marshall & Co., 1867

Suggestions for the reform of the electoral system with a simple form of proportional representation

Photography Made Easy, 1872

'Barometrical and Thermometrical Clocks for Registering Mean Atmospheric Pressure and Temperature' Journal of the Meteorological Society 3, 1877

Experimental Researches into the Properties nad Motions of Fluids, E and F Spon, 1881.

This is a book of 550 pages. Professor John Tyndall, of the Royal Institution, wrote "It fills me with wonder that a man otherwise so occupied should be able to produce a work involving such enormous labour", and on 21st December he received a letter from Charles Darwin commenting on certain passages.

Stanley's Pretty Figure Book, Macmillan, Adams & Co., 1881

Adding is more comprehensible to very small children than multiplication is and this book was intended to help them to understand multiplication through adding.

'A Suggestion for the Improvement of Radiation Thermometers' Journal of the Meteorological Society 11, 1885

'On Three Years Work with the Chrono-barometer and Chrono-thermometer, 1882-84' ibid 12, 1886

'A Simple Snow-gauge', ibid

'The Stature of the Human Race' Nature 36, 1887

Surveying and Levelling Instruments Theoretically and Practically Described, E & F Spon, 1890.

Reviewed in many technical magazines: Colliery Guardian, Colliery Manager, Engineer, Estates Gazette, British Architect, Mining World, Athenaeum and others.

Essay 'Upon the improbability of the theory that former glacial periods in the Northern hemisphere were due to eccentricity of the earth's orbit and to its winter perihelion in the North'.

'Note on a New Spirometer' Journal of the Anthropological Institute 20, 1891

Notes on the Nebular Theory in Relation to Stellar, Solar, Planetary, Cometary and Geological Phenomena, Kegan Paul, Trench & Co 1895

Joe Smith & His Waxworks: Written by Bill Smith with the help of Mrs Smith and Mr Saunders (WFS) and with Pictures by Mr Pitcher, Neville Beeman, Ltd., 1896.

This could be described as "faction". It portrays the life of travelling fairground people with fictional characters but the principal purpose seems to be to demonstrate the harsh treatment meted out to children before the days of compulsory education.

The Case of The. Fox: Being his Prophecies under Hypnosis of the period ending A.D. 1950, alternatively titled simply Utopia, Truslove & Hanson, 1903.

This is an idiosyncratic book with an idiosyncratic title, for "The." is short for Theodore and Theodore Fox is the fictional character who, under hypnosis, sees the future as Stanley imagines it. A lot of the predictions, or something like them, have come about. He sees Paris as the capital of the United States of Europe, reachable in three hours from London by electric train through a tunnel under the Channel, with a Central Legislative Assembly which conducts most of its work in English, the "most useful and popular language". Much government would still be local to the individual countries.

The House of Lords would be replaced by a Senate. Britain would be a republic, but the Heir to the Throne would have become President. Women would have the vote and there would be 18 women in the House of Commons and 5 in the Senate. However, the function of most women would be to supervise the raising of children. Progressive Income Tax would be at the same level over the whole of Europe, but at quite a low level because wars would no longer happen and defense would not be necessary, so the government would no longer borrow money. But through heavy Death Duties all land would come to belong to the State. There would be an Idlers' Tax on males under 55 who did not work. Work, rather than possessions, would be respected and admired. In fact, there would be public affluence, with magnificent libraries, theatres, museums and sports facilities and no need for anything more than private simplicity.

Transport would be by electric "hotel trains" with a summer line across Siberia linking Europe and America, a Central-European Asiatic Line and trains from north to south in the Americas and Africa. He foresaw no future for air transport, but bigger and better ocean liners which could cross the Atlantic in three days. (This, of course did happen in the 30s to 50s - the Queen Mary took just over four days to do the crossing.) Coal would be exhausted but tidal energy, hydro-electricity, solar power from reflectors and the use of the energy in volcanoes would all be harnessed to provide electricity. Cars would all be electric. Cities would be designed in such a way that the traffic would be at a lower level than the pedestrians.

Telephones would be connected to gramophones to make answering-machines. "Little celluloid cards" would replace money. Machines would have taken over so much work that people would work 5 hours a day, though those with seasonal jobs would be allowed to work 10 hours a day in the season and have corresponding time off at other parts of the year. The money system and the avoirdupois weights and measures would be simplified. Fox-hunting would be banned. Women would have more practical and comfortable clothes. It would be possible to photograph the inside of the body. The educated intelligence of the citizen would be recognised as the best source of national wealth, education would be of supreme importance and crime would automatically decrease with a better understanding by the population of what a civilised society really is. Crime would be considered as an illness and criminals and drunks would be isolated in remote places for a time, murderers for life. On release, those isolated could apply for state protection and be employed on public works.

Procreation is a serious undertaking and only men over 24 and women over 18, in good health and with £50 in the bank (£20 for women) and a clear police record would be allowed to be married and have children, though how this was to be achieved is not explained. Those with congenital defects would not be allowed to be married and would be sent to isolated places, like the criminals, and separated from the opposite sex!

Boys would learn in their youth what they needed to practise as men. A boy leaving school should understand the working of a clock, how gas is made, the principles and effects of electricity, the machine that takes him to town in the morning, the press contrivances by which his paper is printed, the telegraph, the telephone and all around him. He would leave school with knowledge of general mechanics so that he would be qualified to become a refined workman.

This book was reviewed in the Daily News of 23rd November, 1903, but not very favourably. The reviewer finds it "... not particularly commendable either as a vision of any possible future or as a dream of changes immediately desirable".

<u>Turn to the Right</u> or <u>A Plea for a Simple Life</u>, A Comedy in Four Acts, Coventry & Sons, Printers, South Norwood, 1905.

A play performed in the Stanley Hall on May 23/24 1905. The heroine has to fend off numerous suitors when she inherits money and can only assure herself that the man she wants to marry really loves her by making over her money to him before marriage.